ESSAYS IN LOVE

Alain de Botton

ESSAYS IN LOVE

McCLELLAND & STEWART

This edition first published in 2006 by Picador,
an imprint of Pan Macmillan Ltd.

Library and Archives Canada Cataloguing in Publication

De Botton, Alain
Essays in love / Alain de Botton.

ISBN 978-0-7710-2606-5

I. Title.

PR6054.E1324E88 2008   823.914   C2007-904865-X

We acknowledge the financial support of the Government of Canada
through the Book Publishing Industry Development Program and that of
the Government of Ontario through the Ontario Media Development
Corporation's Ontario Book Initiative. We further acknowledge the support
of the Canada Council for the Arts and the Ontario Arts Council for our
publishing program.

Printed and bound in Canada

This book is printed on acid-free paper that is 100% recycled,
ancient-forest friendly (100% post-consumer recycled).

McClelland & Stewart,
a division of Random House of Canada Limited,
A Penguin Random House Company
www.randomhouse.ca

3 4 5   16 15 14

Contents

1

Romantic Fatalism

1. The longing for a destiny is nowhere stronger than in our romantic life. All too often forced to share a bed with those who cannot fathom our soul, can we not be excused for believing (contrary to all the rules of our enlightened age) that we are fated one day to run into the man or woman of our dreams? Can we not be allowed a certain superstitious faith that we will ultimately locate a creature who can appease our painful yearnings? Though our prayers may never be answered, though there may be no end to relationships marked by mutual incomprehension, if the heavens should come to take pity on us, then can we really be expected to attribute our encounter with our prince or princess to a mere coincidence? Or can we not for once escape logic and read it as nothing other than a sign of romantic destiny?

2. One mid-morning in early December, with no thought of love or stories, I was sitting in the economy section of a British Airways jet making its way from Paris to London. We had recently crossed the Normandy coast, where a blanket of winter cloud had given way to an uninterrupted view of

brilliant blue waters. Bored and unable to concentrate, I had picked up the airline magazine, passively imbibing information on resort hotels and airport facilities. There was something comforting about the flight, the dull background throb of the engines, the hushed grey interior, the candy smiles of the airline employees. A trolley carrying a selection of drinks and snacks was making its way down the aisle and, though I was neither hungry nor thirsty, it filled me with the vague anticipation that meals may elicit in aircraft.

3. Morbidly perhaps, the passenger on my left had taken off her headphones in order to study the safety-instruction card placed in the pouch in front of her. It depicted the ideal crash, passengers alighting softly and calmly onto land or water, the ladies taking off their high heels, the children dexterously inflating their vests, the fuselage still intact, the kerosene miraculously non-flammable.

4. 'We're all going to die if this thing screws up, so what are these jokers on about?' asked the passenger, addressing no one in particular.

'I think perhaps it reassures people,' I replied, for I was her only audience.

'Mind you, it's not a bad way to go, very quick, especially if we hit land and you're sitting in the front. I had an uncle who died in a plane crash once. Has anyone you know ever died like that?'

They hadn't, but I had no time to answer for a stewardess arrived and (unaware of the ethical doubts recently cast on her employers) offered us lunch. I requested a glass of orange juice and was going to decline a plate of pale sandwiches when my travelling companion whispered to me, 'Take them anyway. I'll eat yours, I'm starving.'

5.   She had chestnut-coloured hair, cut short so that it left the nape of her neck exposed, and large watery green eyes that refused to look into mine. She was wearing a blue blouse and had placed a grey cardigan over her knees. Her shoulders were slim, almost fragile, and the rawness of her nails showed they were often chewed.

'Are you sure I'm not depriving you?'

'Of course not.'

'I'm sorry, I haven't introduced myself, my name is Chloe,' she announced and extended her hand across the armrest with somewhat touching formality.

An exchange of biography followed. Chloe told me she'd been in Paris in order to attend a trade fair. For the past year, she'd been working as a graphic designer for a fashion magazine in Soho. She'd studied at the Royal College of Art, had been born in York, but moved to Wiltshire as a child, and was now (at the age of twenty-three) living alone in a flat in Islington.

6.   'I hope they haven't lost my luggage,' said Chloe as the plane began to drop towards Heathrow. 'Don't you have that fear, that they'll lose your luggage?'

'I don't think about it, but it's happened to me, twice in fact, once in New York, and once in Frankfurt.'

'God, I hate travelling,' sighed Chloe, and bit the end of her index finger. 'I hate arriving even more, I get real arrival angst. After I've been away for a while, I always think something terrible has happened: all my friends have come together and decided they hate me or my cacti have died.'

'You keep cacti?'

'Several. I went through a cactus phase a while back. Phallic, I know, but I spent a winter in Arizona and sort of got fascinated by them. Do you have any interesting plants?'

'Only an aspidistra, but I do regularly think all my friends might hate me.'

7. The conversation meandered, affording us glimpses of one another's characters, like the brief vistas one catches on a winding mountain road – this before the wheels hit the tarmac, the engines were thrown into reverse, and the plane taxied towards the terminal, where it disgorged its cargo into the crowded immigration hall. By the time I had collected my luggage and passed through customs, I had fallen in love with Chloe.

8. Until one is close to death, it must be difficult to declare anyone as the love of one's life. But only shortly after meeting her, it seemed in no way out of place to think of Chloe in such terms. On our return to London, Chloe and I spent the afternoon together. Then, a week before Christmas, we had dinner in a west London restaurant and, as though it was both the strangest and most natural thing to do, ended the evening in bed. She spent Christmas with her family, I went

to Scotland with friends, but we found ourselves calling one another every day, sometimes as many as five times a day, not to say anything in particular, simply because both of us felt we had never spoken like this to anyone before, that all the rest had been compromise and self-deception, that only now were we finally able to understand and make ourselves understood – that the waiting (quasi-messianic in nature) was truly over. I recognized in her the woman I had clumsily been seeking all my life, a creature whose smile and whose eyes, whose sense of humour and whose taste in books, whose anxieties and whose intelligence miraculously matched those of my ideal.

9. Because I came to feel that we were so right for one another, I grew unable to contemplate the idea that meeting Chloe had simply been a coincidence. I lost the ability to consider the question of predestination with necessary scepticism. Though neither of us had until then been super-stitious, Chloe and I seized upon a host of details, however trivial, as confirmation of what intuitively we felt: *that we had been destined for one another.* We learnt that both of us had been born at around midnight (she at 11.45 p.m., I at 1.15 a.m.) in the same month of an even-numbered year. Both of us had played clarinet and had had parts in school productions of *A Midsummer Night's Dream* (she had played Helena, I an attendant to Theseus). Both of us had two large freckles on the toe of the left foot and a cavity in the same rear molar. Both of us had a habit of sneezing in bright sun-light and of drawing ketchup out of its bottle with a knife.

We even had the same copy of *Anna Karenina* on our shelves (the old Oxford edition) – small details, perhaps, but were these not grounds enough on which believers could found a new religion?

10. We attributed to events a narrative logic they could not inherently have possessed. We mythologized our aircraft encounter into the goddess Aphrodite's design, Act One, Scene One of that primordial narrative, the love story. From the time of each of our births, it seemed as though the giant mind in the sky had been subtly shifting our orbits so that we would one day meet on the Paris–London shuttle. Because love had come true for us, we could overlook the countless stories that fail to occur, romances that never get written because someone misses the plane or loses the phone number. Like historians, we were unmistakably on the side of what had actually happened.

11. We should, of course, have been more sensible. Neither Chloe nor I flew regularly between the two capitals nor had been planning our respective trips for any length of time. Chloe had been sent to Paris at the last minute by her magazine after the deputy editor had happened to fall sick, and I had gone there only because an architectural conference in Bordeaux had finished early enough for me to spend a few days in the capital with a friend. The two national airlines running services between Charles de Gaulle and Heathrow offered us a choice of six flights between nine o'clock and lunchtime on our intended day of return. Given that we

6

both wanted to be back in London by the early afternoon of December 6th, but were unresolved until the very last minute as to what flight we would end up taking, the mathematical probability at dawn of us both being on the same flight (though not necessarily in adjoining seats) had been a figure of one in six.

12.   Chloe later told me that she had intended to take the ten thirty Air France flight, but a bottle of shampoo in her bag had happened to leak as she was checking out of her room, which had meant repacking the bag and wasting a valuable ten minutes. By the time the hotel had produced her bill, cleared her credit card and found her a taxi, it was already nine fifteen, and the chances that she would make the ten thirty Air France flight had receded. When she reached the airport after heavy traffic near the Porte de la Villette, the flight had finished boarding and, because she didn't feel like waiting for the next Air France, she went over to the British Airways terminal, where she booked herself on the ten forty-five plane to London, on which (for my own set of reasons) I happened also to have a seat.

13.   Thereafter, the computer so juggled things that it placed Chloe over the wing of the aircraft in seat 15A and I next to her in seat 15B. What we had ignored when we began speaking over the safety-instruction card was the minuscule probability that our discussion had been reliant upon. As neither of us were likely to fly Club Class, and as there were a hundred and ninety-one economy class seats, and Chloe had

been assigned seat 15A, and I, quite by chance, had been assigned seat 15B, the theoretical probability that Chloe and I would be seated next to one another (though the chances of our actually talking to one another could not be calculated) worked itself out as 220 in 36,290, a figure reducible to a probability of one in 164.955.

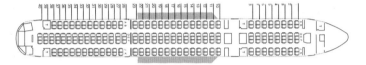

British Airways Boeing 767

14. But this was of course only the probability that we would be seated together if there had been just *one* flight between Paris and London, but as there were six, and as both of us had hesitated between these six, and yet had chosen this one, the probability had to be further multiplied by the original one chance in six, giving a final probability that Chloe and I would meet one December morning over the English Channel in a British Airways Boeing, as one chance in 989.727.

$$P_{flight} = \frac{1}{6}$$

$$P_{seat} = \left(\frac{162}{191} \times \frac{1}{190}\right) + \left(\frac{29}{191} \times \frac{2}{190}\right) = \frac{220}{(191 \times 190)} = \frac{220}{36290} = \frac{1}{164.955}$$

$$P_{flight} \times P_{seat} = \frac{1}{6} \times \frac{220}{36290} = \frac{1}{989.727}$$

15.   And yet it had happened. The calculation, far from convincing us of rational arguments, only backed up the mystical interpretation of our fall into love. If the chances behind an event are enormously remote, yet it occurs nevertheless, may one not be forgiven for invoking a fatalistic explanation? Flicking a coin, a probability of one in two prevents me from turning to God to account for the result. But when it is a question of a probability of one in 989.727, it seemed impossible, from within love at least, that this could have been anything but fate. It would have taken a steady mind to contemplate without superstition the enormous improbability of a meeting that had turned out to alter our lives. Someone (at 30,000 feet) must have been pulling strings in the sky.

16.   From within love, we conceal the chance nature of our lives behind a purposive veil. We insist that the meeting with our redeemer, objectively haphazard and hence unlikely, has been prewritten in a scroll slowly unwinding in the sky. We invent a destiny to spare ourselves the anxiety that would arise from acknowledging that the little sense there is in our lives is merely created by ourselves, that there is no scroll (and hence no preordained fate awaiting) and that who we may or may not be meeting on aeroplanes has no sense beyond that we choose to attribute to it – in short, the anxiety that no one has written our story or assured our loves.

17.   Romantic fatalism protected Chloe and me from the idea that we might equally well have begun loving someone

else had events turned out differently, shocking given how closely love is bound up with a feeling of the necessity and uniqueness of the beloved. How could I have imagined that the role Chloe came to play in my life could equally well have been filled by someone else, when it was with her eyes that I had fallen in love, and her way of draining pasta, combing her hair, and ending a phone conversation?

18.   My mistake was to confuse a destiny to love with a destiny to love a given person. It was the error of thinking that Chloe, rather than love, was inevitable. But my fatalistic interpretation of the start of our story was at least proof of one thing: that I was in love with Chloe. The moment when I would feel that our meeting or not meeting was in the end only an accident, only a probability of one in 989.727, would also be the moment when I would have ceased to feel the absolute necessity of a life with her – and thereby have ceased to love her.

2

Idealization

1. 'Seeing through people is so easy, and it gets you nowhere,' remarked Elias Canetti, suggesting how effortlessly and yet how uselessly we can find fault with others. Do we not fall in love partly out of a momentary will to suspend seeing through people, even at the cost of blinding ourselves a little in the process? If cynicism and love lie at opposite ends of a spectrum, do we not sometimes fall in love in order to escape the debilitating cynicism to which we are prone? Is there not in every coup de foudre a certain wilful exaggeration of the qualities of the beloved, an exaggeration which distracts us from our habitual pessimism and focuses our energies on someone in whom we can believe in a way we have never believed in ourselves?

2. I lost Chloe amidst the throng at passport control, but found her again in the luggage-reclaim area. She was struggling to push a trolley cursed with an inclination to steer to the right, though the Paris carousel was to the far left of the hall. Because my trolley had no mind of its own, I walked over to offer it to her, but she refused, saying one should remain loyal to trolleys, however stubborn, and that

strenuous physical exercise was no bad thing after a flight. Indirectly (via the Karachi arrival), we made it to the Paris carousel, already crowded with faces grown involuntarily familiar since boarding at Charles de Gaulle. The first pieces of luggage had begun to tumble down onto the jointed rubber matting, and faces peered anxiously at the moving display to locate their possessions.

3. 'Have you ever been arrested at customs?' asked Chloe. 'Not yet. Have you?'

'Not really, I once made a confession. This Nazi asked me if I had anything to declare, and I said yes, even though I wasn't carrying anything illegal.'

'So why did you say you were?'

'I don't know, I felt guilty: I have this tendency to confess to things I haven't done. It somehow makes me feel better.'

4. 'By the way, don't judge me on my luggage,' said Chloe as we continued to watch and wait while others got lucky, 'I bought it at the last minute in this discount shop on the Rue de Rennes. It's a bit of a freak.'

'Wait till you see mine. Except that I don't even have an excuse. I've been carrying mine around for over five years.'

'Can I ask you a favour? Could you look after my trolley while I look for the loo? I'll just be a minute. Oh, and if you see a pink carrier bag with a luminous green handle, that'll be mine.'

5. A little later, I watched Chloe walk back towards me across the hall, wearing what I later learnt was her usual pained and slightly anxious expression. She had a face that looked permanently near tears, her eyes carried the fear of a person about to be told a piece of very bad news. Something about her made one want to comfort her, offer her reassurance – or a hand to hold.

6. Love was something I sensed very suddenly, shortly after she had embarked on what promised to be a very long and very boring story (indirectly sparked by the arrival of the Athens flight in the carousel next to us) about a holiday she had taken one summer with her brother in Rhodes. While Chloe talked, I watched her hands fiddling with the belt of her beige woollen coat (a pair of freckles were collected below the index finger) and realized (as if this had been the most self-evident of truths) that I loved her. However awkward it was that she rarely finished her sentences, or was somewhat anxious, and had not perhaps the best taste in earrings, *she was adorable*. I fell prey to a moment of unrestrained idealization, dependent as much on my emotional immaturity as on the elegance of her coat, the after-effects of flying and the depressing interior of the Terminal Four baggage area, against which her beauty showed up so starkly.

7. *The island was packed with tourists, but we rented motorcycles and* . . . Chloe's holiday story was dull, but its dullness no longer counted against it. I had ceased to consider it according to the secular logic of ordinary conversations. I was

no longer concerned to locate within it either insight or humour, what mattered was not so much *what* she was saying, as the fact that *she* was saying it – and that I had decided to find perfection in everything she could utter. I felt ready to follow her into every anecdote (*there was this shop that served fresh olives . . .*), I was ready to love every one of her jokes that had missed its punchline, every reflection that had lost its thread. I felt ready to abandon self-absorption for the sake of consummate empathy, to catalogue every one of Chloe's memories, to become a historian of her childhood, to learn all of her loves and fears. Everything that could possibly have played itself out within her mind and body had promptly grown fascinating.

8. Then the luggage arrived, hers only a few cases behind mine, we loaded it onto the trolleys and walked out through the green channel.

9. What is so frightening is the extent to which we may idealize others when we have such trouble tolerating ourselves – *because* we have such trouble . . . I must have realized that Chloe was only human, with all the implications carried by the word, but could I not be forgiven for my desire to suspend such a thought? Every fall into love involves the triumph of hope over self-knowledge. We fall in love hoping we won't find in another what we know is in ourselves, all the cowardice, weakness, laziness, dishonesty, compromise, and stupidity. We throw a cordon of love around the chosen one and decide that everything within it will somehow be

free of our faults. We locate inside another a perfection that eludes us within ourselves, and through our union with the beloved, hope to maintain (against the evidence of all self-knowledge) a precarious faith in our species.

10. Why did this awareness not prevent my fall into love? Because the illogicality and childishness of my desire did not outweigh my need to believe. I knew the void that romantic intoxication could fill, I knew the exhilaration that comes from identifying someone, anyone, as admirable. Long before I had even laid eyes on Chloe, I must have needed to find in the face of another an integrity I had never caught sight of within myself.

11. 'May I check your bags sir?' asked the customs man. 'Do you have anything to declare, any alcohol, cigarettes, firearms . . . ?'

Like Oscar Wilde with his genius, I wanted to say, '*Only my love,*' but my love was not a crime, not yet at least.

'Shall I wait with you?' asked Chloe.

'Are you together with madam?' enquired the customs officer.

Afraid of presumption, I answered no, but asked Chloe if she'd wait for me on the other side of the border.

12. Love reinvents our needs with unique speed. My impatience with the customs ritual indicated that Chloe, who I had not known existed a few hours ago, had already acquired the status of a craving. I felt I would die if I missed

her outside – die for the sake of someone who had only entered my life at eleven thirty that morning.

13. Chloe had waited, but we could spend only a moment together. She had parked her car nearby. I had to take a taxi to my office. Both parties hesitated whether or not to continue with the story.

'I'll give you a call some time,' I said casually, 'we could go and buy some luggage together.'

'That's a good idea,' said Chloe, 'have you got my number?'

'I'm afraid I already memorized it, it was written on your baggage tag.'

'You'd make a good detective, I hope your memory is up to it. Well, it was nice meeting you,' said Chloe extending a hand.

'Good luck with the cacti,' I called after her as I watched her head for the lifts, her trolley still veering insanely to the right.

14. In the taxi on the way into town, I felt a curious sense of loss. Could this really be love? To speak of love after we had barely spent a morning together was to encounter charges of romantic delusion and semantic folly. Yet we can perhaps only ever fall in love without knowing quite who we have fallen in love with. The initial convulsion is necessarily founded on ignorance. Love or simple obsession? Who, if not time (which lies in its own way), could possibly begin to tell?

3

The Subtext of Seduction

1. For those in love with certainty, seduction is no territory in which to stray. Every smile and word lead to a dozen if not twelve thousand possibilities. Remarks that in normal life (that is, life without love) can be taken at face value now exhaust dictionaries with their possible meanings. And for the seducer, the doubts reduce themselves to a central question, faced with the trepidation of a criminal awaiting sentence: *Does s/he, or does s/he not, desire me?*

2. The thought of Chloe did not stop haunting me in the days that followed our encounter. Though under pressure to complete plans for an office building near King's Cross, my mind drifted irresponsibly but irresistibly back to her. I felt the need to circle around the object of my adoration, she kept breaking into consciousness with the urgency of a matter that had to be addressed, though my thoughts had no point to them, they were (objectively speaking) utterly devoid of interest. Some of these Chloe-dreams ran like this, *'Oh, how sweet she is, how nice it would be to . . .'*
Others were more visual:

(i)   Chloe framed by the aircraft window

(ii)   Her watery green eyes

(iii)   Her teeth biting briefly into her lower lip

(iv)   The tilt of her neck when yawning

(v)   The gap between her two front teeth

3.   If only I had summoned such diligence for her phone number, for the digits had altogether evaporated from my memory (a memory that felt its time better spent replaying images of Chloe's lower lip). Was it *(071)*

> *607 9187*
>> *609 7187*
>>> *601 7987*
>>>> *690 7187*
>>>>> *610 7987*
>>>>>> *670 9817*
>>>>>>> *687 7187*   ?

4. The search began badly. *607 9187* was not the beloved's abode but a funeral parlour off Upper Street, though the establishment didn't reveal itself to be one until the end of a trying conversation, in the course of which I learnt that After Life also had an employee called Chloe, who was summoned to the phone and spent agonizing minutes trying to place my name (eventually identifying me as a customer who had made inquiries into urns) before the confusion of names was cleared up and I hung up, red-faced, drenched with sweat, nearer death than life.

5. When I finally reached my Chloe at work the following day, she too seemed to have relegated me to the next world. 'Things are crazy around here now. Can you hold for a minute?' she asked secretarially.

I held, offended. Whatever intimacy I had imagined, back in office space, we were strangers.

'Listen, I'm sorry,' she said, coming back on the line, 'I can't talk now, we're rushing to get a supplement off to press tomorrow. Can I call you back? I'll try to reach you either at home or in the office when things calm down.'

6. The telephone becomes an instrument of torture in the demonic hands of a beloved who doesn't ring. When Chloe called a few days later, I had rehearsed my speech too often to deliver it correctly. I was caught unprepared, hanging socks on a rail. I ran to the bedroom to pick up. My voice carried with it a tension and an anger that I might more skilfully have erased from a page. Authorship becomes tempting to those who can't speak.

'What a surprise to hear from you,' I said unconvincingly. 'We must have lunch some time.'

'Lunch. Goodness. I really can't this week.'

'Well, how about dinner?'

'I'm just looking at my diary, and you're not going to believe this, but that's looking difficult too.'

'No problem,' I said, in a tone that strongly implied its opposite.

'I tell you what, though, can you take this afternoon off

by any chance? We could meet at my office and go to the National Gallery or something.'

7. The questions did not let up. What did Chloe think as we made our way to Trafalgar Square from her office in Bedford Street? On the one hand, she had been happy to take the afternoon off to tour a museum with a man she'd only briefly met on an aeroplane over a week before. But on the other hand, there was nothing in her behaviour to suggest that this was anything but an opportunity for a friendly discussion. Suspended between innocence and collusion, Chloe's every gesture became imbued with maddening significance. Was I correct to detect traces of flirtation at the ends of her sentences and the corners of her smiles, or was this merely my own desire projected onto the face of innocence?

8. We began our visit with the early Italians, though my thoughts (I had lost all perspective, they had yet to find theirs) were not with them. Before *The Virgin and Child with Saints*, Chloe turned to remark that she had always had a thing about Signorelli and, because it seemed appropriate, I invented a passion for Antonello's *Christ Crucified*. She looked thoughtful, immersed in the canvases, oblivious to the noise and activity in the gallery. I followed a few paces behind her, trying to focus on the paintings, but able only to look at her looking.

In the second and more crowded Italian room (1500–1600), we stood so close together that my hand suddenly touched hers. She didn't draw away and for a moment the feel of her skin tingled through me. We faced a painting by Bronzino, *An Allegory of Venus and Cupid*. Cupid kisses his mother Venus, who surreptitiously removes one of his arrows: beauty blinding love.

9. Then, brusquely, as though an error had promptly come to light, the hand moved away.

'I love those little figures in the background, the little nymphs and angry gods and stuff,' said Chloe. 'Do you understand all the symbolism?'

'Not really, besides it being Venus and Cupid.'

'I didn't even know that, so you're one up on me. I wish I'd read more about ancient mythology,' she continued. 'But actually, I like looking at things and not knowing quite what they mean.'

She turned to face the painting, her hand once more brushing against mine.

10. Was the hand a symbol (subtler than Bronzino's and less well documented) of desire or the innocent, unconscious spasm of a tired arm muscle? What was I to make of the way Chloe straightened her skirt as we crossed into Early Northern Painting or coughed by van Eyck's *The Marriage of Giovanni Arnolfini* or handed me the catalogue in order to rest her head on her hand?

Desire had turned me into a relentless hunter for clues, a romantic paranoiac, *reading meaning into everything*. But whatever my impatience with the rituals of seduction, I was aware that the enigma lent Chloe a distinctive appeal. The most attractive are not those who allow us to kiss them at once (we soon feel ungrateful) or those who never allow us to kiss them (we soon forget them), but those who know how carefully to administer varied doses of hope and despair.

11.   Venus felt like a drink, so she and Cupid headed for the lifts. In the cafeteria, Chloe took a tray and pushed it down the steel runway.

'Do you want tea?' she asked.

'Yeah, but I'll get it.'

'Don't be silly, I'll get it.'

'Please let me do it.'

'No, no, I will.'

The game continued for a few more rounds, its vigour apparently accounted for by a mutual, irrational anxiety about the commitment involved in letting someone else pay for a drink. We sat at a table with a view of Trafalgar Square, the lights of the Christmas tree lending an eerily festive atmosphere to the urban scene. We began talking of art, then moved on to artists, and from artists, we went to get a second cup of tea (she won) and a cake (2–1), then we digressed on to beauty, and from beauty we went to love.

'I don't understand,' said Chloe, 'you do or you don't think that there's such a thing as true love?'

'I'm saying it's very subjective. You can't suppose that there's one quality called "love", people mean such different things by the word. It's tricky to distinguish between passion and love, infatuation and love—'

'Don't you find this cake disgusting?' interrupted Chloe.

'We should never have bought it. I mean, you shouldn't have bought it for me. God, I'm so rude.'

'I'll be expecting a written apology.'

'But seriously, if you asked most people whether they believed in love or not, they'd probably say they didn't. Yet that's not necessarily what they truly think. It's just the way they defend themselves against what they want. They believe in it, but pretend they don't until they're allowed to. Most people would throw away all their cynicism if they could. The majority just never get the chance.'

12.   Who were these 'most people' she talked of? Was *I* the man who would dispel her cynicism? We talked abstractly of love, ignoring that lying on the table was not the nature of love per se but the burning question of who we were and would be to one another.

Or was there in fact nothing on the table other than a half-eaten carrot cake and two cups of tea? Was Chloe being as abstract as she wished, meaning precisely what she said, the diametrical opposite of the first rule of flirtation, where what is said is never what is meant?

13.   Our hesitancy was a game, but a serious and useful one, which minimized offending an unwilling partner and eased a willing one more slowly into the prospect of mutual desire. The threat of the great 'I like you' could be softened by adding, 'but not so much that I will let you know it directly . . .' Chloe and I were politely sparing each other the need to pay the full price for a candid declaration of love.

14.   We helped to define what we wanted by reference to others. Chloe had a friend at work who had a history of relationships with unsuitable types. A courier was the current blunderer.

'I mean, why does she hang out with a burly bloke in leather trousers who smells of exhaust fumes and is using her for sex? And that's fine if she wanted to use him for sex too, but apparently he can't even sustain an erection for that long.'

'How terrible,' I answered, worried by the possible definition of the word 'long'.

'Or just sad. One has to go into relationships with equal expectations, ready to give as much as the other – not with one person wanting a fling and the other real love. I think that's where all the agony comes from.'

15.   Because it was past six and her office was closing, I asked Chloe whether she might not after all be free to have dinner with me that night. She smiled at the suggestion, stared briefly out of the window at a bus heading past St Martin-in-the-Fields, looked back and said, 'No, thanks, that would really be impossible.'

Then, just as I was ready to despair, she blushed.

16.   Faced with ambiguous signals, what better explanation than shyness: *the beloved desires, but is too shy to say so.* The seducer who wishes to call his victim shy will never be disappointed.

'My God, I've just forgotten something terrible,' said

Chloe, offering an alternative explanation for a red face, 'I was supposed to call the printer this afternoon. I can't believe I forgot to do that. I'm losing my head.'

The lover offered sympathy.

'But look, about dinner, we'll have to do it another time. I'd love that, I really would. It's just difficult at the moment, but I'll give my diary another look and call you tomorrow, I promise I will, and maybe we can fix something up for before this weekend.'

4

Authenticity

1. It is one of the ironies of love that it is easiest confidently to seduce those to whom we are least attracted. My feelings for Chloe meant I lost any belief in my own worthiness. Who could *I* be next to *her*? Was it not the greatest honour for her to have agreed to this dinner, to have dressed so elegantly ('Is this all right?' she'd asked in the car on the way to the restaurant, 'It had better be, because I'm not changing a sixth time'), let alone that she might be willing to respond kindly to some of the things that might fall (if ever I recovered my tongue) from my unworthy lips?

2. It was Friday night and Chloe and I were seated at a corner table of Les Liaisons Dangereuses, a French restaurant that had recently opened at the end of the Fulham Road. There could have been no more appropriate setting for Chloe's beauty. The chandeliers threw soft shadows across her face, the light green walls matched her light green eyes. And yet, as though struck dumb by the angel that faced me across the table, I lost all capacity either to think or speak and could only silently draw invisible patterns on the starched white

tablecloth and take unnecessary sips of bubbled water from a large glass goblet.

3. My sense of inferiority bred a need to take on a personality that was not my own, a seducing self that would respond to every demand and suggestion made by my exalted companion. Love forced me to look at myself as though through Chloe's imagined eyes. 'Who could I become to please her?' I wondered. I did not tell flagrant lies, I simply attempted to anticipate everything I believed she might want to hear.

'Would you like some wine?' I asked her.

'I don't know, would you like wine?' she asked back.

'I really don't mind, if you feel like it,' I replied.

'It's as you please, whatever you want,' she continued. 'Either way is fine with me.'

'I agree.'

'So should we have it or not?'

'Well, I don't think *I'll* have any,' ventured Chloe.

'You're right, I don't feel like any either,' I concurred.

'Let's not have wine, then,' she concluded.

'Great, so we'll just stick with the water.'

4. The first course arrived, arranged on plates with the symmetry of a formal French garden.

'It looks too beautiful to touch,' said Chloe (how I knew the feeling), 'I've never eaten grilled scallops like this before.'

We began to eat. The only sound was that of cutlery

against china. There seemed to be nothing to say. Chloe had been my only thought for too long, but the one thought that at this moment I could not share with her.

Silence was damning. A silence with an unattractive person implies they are the boring one. A silence with an attractive one immediately renders it certain *you* are the tedious party.

5. Silence and clumsiness could of course be taken as rather pitiful proof of desire. It being easy enough to seduce someone towards whom one feels indifferent, the clumsiest seducers could generously be deemed the most genuine. Not to find the right words is paradoxically often the best proof that the right words are meant. In that other *Liaisons Dangereuses*, the Marquise de Merteuil faults the Vicomte de Valmont for writing love letters that are too perfect, too logical to be the words of a true lover, whose thoughts will be disjointed and for whom the fine phrase will always elude. Real desire lacks articulacy – but how willingly I would at that moment have swapped my constipation for the Vicomte's loquacity.

6. I had to find out more about Chloe, for how could I abandon my true self unless I knew what false self to adopt? But the patience and intelligence required to fathom someone else went far beyond the capacities of my anxious, infatuated mind. I behaved like a reductive social psychologist, eager to press my companion into simple categories, unwilling to apply the care of a novelist to capturing the

subtleties of human nature. Over the first course, I blundered with heavy-handed, interview-like questions: What do you like to read? (*'Joyce, Henry James, Cosmo if there's time'*), Do you like your job? (*'All jobs are pretty crap, don't you think?'*), What country would you live in if you could live anywhere? (*'I'm fine here, anywhere where I don't have to change the plug for my hairdryer'*), What do you like to do on weekends? (*'Go to the movies on Saturday, on Sunday, stock up on chocolate for getting depressed with in the evening'*).

7.   Behind such clumsy questions (with every one I asked, I seemed to get further from knowing her) rested an impatient attempt to get to the most direct question of all, *'Who are you?'* – and hence *'Who should I be?'* But my directness was doomed, and the more I practised it, the more my subject escaped through the net, letting me know what newspaper she read and music she liked, but not thereby enlightening me as to who she might really be.

8.   Chloe hated talking about herself. Perhaps her most obvious feature was a certain modesty and self-deprecation. When the conversation led her to refer to herself, it would not simply be 'I' or 'Chloe', but *'a basket-case like me'*. Her self-deprecation was all the more attractive for it seemed to be free of the veiled appeals of self-pitying people, the false self-deprecation of the *I'm so stupid / No, you're not* school.

Her childhood had been awkward, but she was stoic about the matter (*'I hate childhood dramatizations that make Job look like he got off lightly'*). She had grown up in a financially comfortable home. Her father (*'All his problems started when his parents called him Barry'*) had been an academic, a law professor, her mother (*'Claire'*) had for a time run a flower shop. Chloe was the middle child, a girl sandwiched between two favoured and faultless boys. When her older brother died of leukaemia shortly after her eighth birthday, her parents' grief expressed itself as anger at their daughter who, slow at school and sulky around the house, had obstinately clung to life instead of their son. She grew up guilty, filled with a sense of blame for what had happened, feelings that her mother did little to alleviate. The mother liked to pick on a person's weakest characteristics and not let go. Chloe was forever reminded of how badly she performed at school compared to her dead brother, of how gauche she was, and of how disreputable her friends were (criticisms that were not particularly true, but that grew more so with every mention). Chloe had turned to her father for affection, but the man was as closed with his emotions as he was open with his legal knowledge, which he would pedantically share with her as a substitute for warmth, until her adolescence when Chloe's frustration with him turned to anger and she openly defied him and everything he stood for (it was fortunate that I had not chosen the legal profession).

9. Of past boyfriends, only hints emerged over the meal: one had worked as motorcycle mechanic in Italy and had treated her badly, another, who she had mothered, had ended up in jail for possession of drugs. A third had been an analytical philosopher at London University (*'You don't have to be Freud*

to see he was the daddy I never went to bed with'), a fourth a test-car driver for Rover ('*To this day I can't explain that one. I think I liked his Birmingham accent*'). But no clear picture was emerging and therefore the shape of her ideal man forming in my head needed constant readjustment. There were things she praised and condemned within sentences, forcing me into frantic rewriting. At one moment she seemed to be praising emotional vulnerability, and at the next, damning it in favour of independence. Whereas honesty was at one point extolled as the supreme value, adultery was at another justified on account of the greater hypocrisy of marriage.

10. The complexity of her views led to a schizophrenia in mine. The main course (duck for me, salmon for her) was a marshland sowed with mines. Did I think two people should live solely for one another? Had my childhood been difficult? Had I ever been truly in love? Was I an emotional or a cere-bral person? Who had I voted for in the last election? What was my favourite colour? Did I think women were more unstable than men? Because it involves the risk of alienating those who don't agree with what one is saying, originality proved wholly beyond me.

11. Chloe was facing a different dilemma, for it was time for dessert, and though she had only one choice, she had more than one desire.

'What do you think, the chocolate or the caramel?' she asked, traces of guilt appearing on her forehead. 'Maybe you can get one and I'll get the other and then we can share.'

I felt like neither, I was not digesting properly, but that wasn't the point.

'I just love chocolate, don't you?' asked Chloe. 'I can't understand people who don't like chocolate. I was once going out with a guy, this guy Robert I was telling you about, and I was never really comfortable with him, but I couldn't work out why. Then one day it all became clear: *he didn't like chocolate*. I mean he didn't just not love it, this guy actually hated it. You could have put a bar in front of him and he wouldn't have touched it. That kind of thinking is so far removed from anything I can relate to, you know. Well, after that, you can imagine, it was clear we had to break up.'

'In that case we should get both desserts and taste each other's. But which one do you prefer?'

'I don't mind,' lied Chloe.

'Really? Well if you don't mind, then I'll take the chocolate, I just can't resist it. In fact, you see the double chocolate cake at the bottom there? I think I'll order that. It looks far more chocolaty.'

'You're being seriously sinful,' said Chloe, biting her lower lip in a mixture of anticipation and shame, 'but why not? You're absolutely right. Life is short and all that.'

12. Yet again I had lied (I was beginning to hear the sounds of cocks crowing in the kitchen). I had been more or less allergic to chocolate all my life, but how could I have been honest when the love of chocolate had been so conclusively identified as a criterion of Chloe-compatibility?

I had decided that attraction was synonymous with the

removal of all personal characteristics, my true self being necessarily in conflict with, and unworthy of the perfections found in the beloved.

13. I had lied, but did Chloe like me any the more for it? Curiously, she merely expressed a certain disappointment, in view of the inferior taste of caramel, that I should have insisted so strongly on taking the chocolate – adding in an off-hand way that a chocophile was in the end perhaps as much of a problem as a chocophobe.

14. We charm by coincidence rather than design. What had Chloe done to make me fall in love with her? My feelings had as much to do with the adorable way she had asked the waiter for extra butter as they had to do with her views on politics or the dress she had carefully chosen.

The steps I had on occasion seen women take to seduce me were rarely the ones I had responded to. I was more likely to be attracted by tangential details that the seducer had not even been sufficiently aware of to push to the fore. I had once taken to a woman who had a trace of down on her upper lip. Normally squeamish about this, I had mysteriously been charmed by it in her case, my desire stubbornly deciding to collect there rather than around her warm smile or intelligent conversation. When I discussed my attraction with friends, I struggled to suggest that it had to do with an indefinable 'aura' – but I could not disguise to myself that I had fallen in love with a hairy upper lip. When I saw the woman again, someone must have suggested electrolysis, for the down was gone, and (despite her many qualities) my desire soon followed suit.

15.   The Euston Road was still blocked with traffic when we made our way back towards Islington. Long before such issues could have become meaningful, we'd arranged that I would drop Chloe home, but nevertheless the dilemmas of seduction remained a weighty presence in the car. At some point in the game, the actor must risk losing his audience. However, reaching the door of 23a Liverpool Road, awed by the dangers of misreading the signs, I concluded that the moment to propose metaphorical coffee had not yet arisen.

But after such a tense and chocolate-rich meal, my stomach suddenly developed different priorities, and I was forced to ask to be allowed up to the flat. I followed Chloe up the stairs, into the living room and was directed to the bathroom. Emerging a few minutes later with my intentions unaltered, I reached for my coat and announced, with all the thoughtful authority of a man who has decided restraint would be best and fantasies entertained in weeks previous should remain just that, that I had spent a lovely evening, hoped to see her again soon and would call her after the Christmas holidays. Pleased with such maturity, I kissed her on both cheeks, wished her goodnight and turned to leave the flat.

16.   It was therefore fortunate that Chloe was not so easily persuaded, arresting my flight by the ends of my scarf. She drew me back into the apartment, placed both arms around

me and, looking me firmly in the eye with a grin she had previously reserved for the idea of chocolate, whispered, 'We're not children, you know.' And with these words, she placed her lips on mine and we embarked on one of the longer and more beautiful kisses mankind has ever known.

5

Mind and Body

1. Few things are as antithetical to sex as thought. Sex is instinctive, unreflexive and spontaneous, while thought is careful, uninvolved, and judgemental. To think during sex is to violate a fundamental law of intercourse. But did I have a choice?

2. It was the sweetest kiss, everything one dreams a kiss might be. It began with a light grazing and tender tentative forays that secreted the unique flavour of our skins. Then the pressure increased, our lips rejoined and parted, mine leaving Chloe's for a moment in order to run along her cheeks, her temples, her ears. She pressed her body closer and our legs intertwined. Dizzy, we collapsed onto the sofa, clutching at one another.

3. Yet if there was something interrupting this Eden, it was the awareness of how strange it was for me to be lying in Chloe's living room, my lips on hers, feeling her heat beside me. After all the ambiguity, the kiss had come so suddenly that my mind now refused to cede control of events to the

body. It was the thought of the kiss, rather than the kiss itself, that was holding my attention.

4. I couldn't help but think that a woman whose body had but a few hours ago been an area of complete privacy (only suggested by the outlines of her blouse and the contours of her skirt) was now preparing to undress before me. Though we had talked at length, I felt a disproportion between my day-time and night-time knowledge of Chloe, between the intimacy that contact with her body implied and the largely unknown realms of the rest of her life. But the presence of such thoughts, flowing in conjunction with our physical breathlessness, seemed to run rudely counter to the laws of desire. They seemed to be ushering in an unpleasant degree of objectivity, like a third person who would watch, observe, and perhaps even judge.

5. 'Wait,' said Chloe as I unbuttoned her blouse, 'I'm going to draw the curtains, I don't want the whole street to see. Or why don't we move into the bedroom? We'll have more space.'

We picked ourselves up from the cramped sofa and walked down a book-lined corridor into Chloe's bedroom. A large white bed stood in the centre, piled high with cushions and papers, clothes, and a telephone.

'Excuse the mess,' said Chloe, 'the rest of the place is just for show, this is where I really live.'

There was an animal on top of the mess.

'Meet Guppy – my first love,' said Chloe, handing me a furry grey elephant whose face bore no signs of jealousy.

6. There was an awkwardness while Chloe cleared the surface of the bed, the eagerness of our bodies only a minute before had given way to a heavy silence that indicated how uncomfortably close we were to our own nakedness.

7. When Chloe and I undressed one another on top of the large white bed and, by the light of a small bedside lamp, saw each other naked for the first time, we attempted to be as unselfconscious as Adam and Eve before the Fall. I slipped my hands under Chloe's skirt and she unbuttoned my trousers with an air of indifferent normality, like someone opening the post or changing a duvet.

8. But if there was one thing likely to check our passion, it was clumsiness. It was clumsiness that reminded Chloe and me of the humour and bizarreness of having ended up in bed together, I struggling to peel off her underwear (some of it had become caught around her knees), she having trouble with the buttons of my shirt – yet each of us trying not to comment, not to smile even, looking at one another with an earnest air of desire, as though oblivious to the potentially comic side of what was going on, sitting semi-naked on the edge of the bed, our faces flushed like those of guilty schoolchildren.

9. The philosopher in the bedroom is as ludicrous a figure

as the philosopher in the nightclub. In both arenas, because the body is predominant and vulnerable, the mind becomes an instrument of silent, uninvolved assessment. Thought's infidelity lies in its privacy. *'If there is something that you cannot say to me,'* asks the lover, *'things that you must think alone, then can you really be trusted?'*

I wasn't thinking anything cruel while I ran my hands and lips across Chloe's body, it was simply that Chloe would probably have been disturbed by news that I was thinking at all. Because thought implies judgement, and because we are all paranoid enough to take judgement to be negative, it is constitutionally suspect in the bedroom. Hence the sighing that drowns the sounds of lovers' thoughts, sighing that confirms: *I am too passionate to be thinking.* I kiss, and therefore I do not think – such is the official myth under which lovemaking takes place, the bedroom a unique space in which partners tacitly agree not to remind one another of the awe-inspiring wonder of their nudity.

10.   There is the story of a nineteenth-century pious young virgin who, on the day of her wedding, was warned by her mother, 'Tonight, it will seem your husband has gone mad, but you will find he has recovered by morning.' Is the mind not offensive precisely because it symbolizes a refusal of this insanity, seeming like an unfair way of keeping one's head while others are losing their breath?

11.   In the course of what Masters and Johnson have called a plateau period, Chloe looked up at me and asked,

'What are you thinking about, Socrates?'

'Nothing,' I answered.

'Bullshit, I can see it in your eyes, what are you smiling about?'

'Nothing, I tell you, or else everything, a thousand things, you, the evening, how we ended up here, how strange and yet comfortable it feels.'

'Strange?'

'I don't know, yes, strange, I suppose I'm being absurdly self-conscious about things.'

Chloe laughed.

'What's so funny?'

'Turn round for a second.'

'Why?'

'Just turn over.'

On one side of the room, positioned over a chest of drawers and angled so it had been in Chloe's field of vision, was a large mirror that showed both of our bodies lying together, entangled in the bed linen.

Had Chloe been watching us all the while?

'I'm sorry, I should have told you,' she smiled, 'it's just I didn't want to ask – not on the first night. It might have made you self-conscious.'

6

Marxism

1. When we look at someone (an angel) from a position of unrequited love and imagine the pleasures that being in heaven with them might bring us, we are prone to overlook a significant danger: how soon their attractions might pale if they began to love us back. We fall in love because we long to escape from ourselves with someone as ideal as we are corrupt. But what if such a being were one day to turn around and love us back? We can only be shocked. How could they be divine as we had hoped when they have the bad taste to approve of someone like us? If in order to love, we must believe that the beloved surpasses us in some way, does not a cruel paradox emerge when we witness this love returned? *'If s/he really is so wonderful, how could s/he could love someone like* me*?'*

2. There is no richer territory for students of romantic psychology than the atmosphere of the morning after. But Chloe had other priorities upon stumbling out of sleep. She went to wash her hair in the bathroom next door and I awoke to hear water crashing on tiles. I remained in bed, encasing myself in the shape and smell of her body that lingered in

the sheets. It was Saturday morning, and the timid rays of a December sun were filtering through the curtains. It was a privilege to be curled up in Chloe's inner sanctum, looking at the objects that made up her daily life, at the walls she woke to every morning, at her alarm clock, a packet of aspirins, her watch and her earrings on the bedside table. My love manifested itself as a fascination for everything Chloe owned, for the material signs of a life I had yet fully to discover but that seemed infinitely rich, full of the wonder the everyday takes on in the hands of an extraordinary being. There was a bright yellow radio in one corner, a print by Matisse was leaning against a chair, her clothes from the night before were hanging in the closet by the mirror. On the chest of drawers there was a pile of paperbacks, next to it, her handbag and keys, a bottle of mineral water and Guppy the elephant. By a form of transference, I fell in love with everything she owned, it all seemed so intriguing, tasteful, different from what one could ordinarily buy in the shops.

3. 'Have you been trying on my underwear?' asked Chloe a moment later, emerging from the bathroom wrapped in a fluffy white robe and a towel around her head. 'What have you been doing all this time? You have to get out of bed, we can't waste our day.'

I sighed playfully.

'I'm going to go and prepare us some breakfast, so why don't you have a shower in the meantime. There's some clean towels in the cupboard. And how about a kiss?'

4. The bathroom was another chamber of wonders, full of jars, lotions, and perfumes: the shrine of her body, my visit a watery pilgrimage. I washed my hair, sang like a hyena beneath the cascade, dried myself, and made use of a new toothbrush Chloe had given me. When I returned to the bedroom some fifteen minutes later, she was gone, the bed was made, the room tidied and the curtains opened.

5. Chloe had not just made toast, she'd prepared a feast. There was a basket of croissants, orange juice, a pot of fresh coffee, some eggs and toast, and a huge bowl of yellow and red flowers in the centre of the table.

6. 'It's fantastic,' I said, 'you prepared all this in the time it took me to have a shower and get dressed.'

'That's because I'm not lazy like you. Come on, let's eat before everything gets cold.'

'You're so sweet to have done this.'

'Rubbish.'

'No seriously, you are. It's not every day I get breakfast cooked for me,' I said, and put my arms around her waist. She didn't turn to look at me, but took my hand in hers and squeezed it for a moment.

'Don't flatter yourself, it's not for you I did this, I eat like this every weekend.'

Her lie was symptomatic of a certain pride she took in mocking the romantic, in being unsentimental, matter of fact, stoic, yet at heart, she was the opposite: idealistic, dreamy, giving, and deeply attached to everything she liked verbally to dismiss as *mushy*.

7. In the course of a supremely *mushy* breakfast, I realized something that might perhaps have seemed obvious, but that struck me as both unexpected and complicated: that Chloe had begun to feel for me a little of what I had for many weeks felt for her. Objectively, this was not an unusual thought, but in falling in love with her, I had somehow entirely overlooked the possibility of reciprocation. I had counted more on loving than being loved. And if I had concentrated largely on the former dynamic, it was perhaps because being loved is always the more complicated of the two emotions, Cupid's arrow easier to send than receive.

8. It was this difficulty of receiving that struck me over breakfast, for though the croissants could not have been more buttery and the coffee more aromatic, something about the attention and affection they symbolized disturbed me. Chloe had opened her body to me the night before, in the morning she had opened her kitchen, but I could not now prevent a sense of uneasiness, that bordered on irritation, and amounted to the muffled thought: *'What have I done to deserve this?'*

9. If one is not wholly convinced of one's own lovability, receiving affection can appear like being bestowed an honour for a feat one feels no connection with. Lovers unfortunate

enough to prepare breakfast for such types must brace themselves for the recriminations due to all false flatterers.

10.   What arguments are about is never as important as the
discomfort for which they are an excuse. Ours started over
strawberry jam.

'Do you have any strawberry jam?' I asked Chloe, sur-
veying the laden table.

'No, but there's raspberry here, do you mind?'

'Sort of, yes.'

'Well, there's blackberry as well.'

'I hate blackberry, do you like blackberry?'

'Yeah, why not?'

'It's horrible. So there's no decent jam?'

'I wouldn't put it quite like that. There's five pots of jam
on the table, there's just no strawberry.'

'I see.'

'Why are you making such a big deal of it?'

'Because I hate having breakfast without decent jam.'

'But there is decent jam, just not the one you like.'

'Is the shop far?'

'Why?'

'I am going out to buy some.'

'For Christ's sake, we've just sat down, everything will
be cold if you go now.'

'I'll go.'

'Why, if everything's going to get cold?'

'Because I need jam, that's why.'

'What's up with you?'

'Nothing, why?'

'You're being ridiculous.'

'No, I'm not.'

'Yes you are.'

'I just need jam.'

'Why are you being so impossible? I've cooked you this whole breakfast and all you can do is make a fuss about some pot of jam. If you really want your jam, just get the hell out of here and eat it in someone else's company.'

11. There was a silence, Chloe's eyes glazed, then abruptly she stood up and walked into the bedroom, slamming the door behind her. I remained at the table, listening to what might have been crying, feeling like a fool for upsetting the woman I claimed to love.

12. Unrequited love may be painful, but it is safely painful, because it does not involve inflicting damage on anyone but oneself, a private pain that is as bitter-sweet as it is self-induced. But as soon as love is reciprocated, one must be prepared to give up the passivity of simply *being* hurt to take on the responsibility of perpetrating hurt oneself.

13. The repugnance I felt towards myself for hurting Chloe was momentarily turned against her. I hated her for all the efforts she had made with me, for her weakness in believing in me, for her bad taste in allowing me to upset her. It suddenly seemed pitiable that she had given me her toothbrush, prepared breakfast for me, and begun to cry in the bedroom

like a child. I gave way to an overwhelming urge to punish her for her weakness.

14.   What had turned me into such a monster? The fact that I had always been something of a Marxist.

15.   There is the old joke made by the Marx who laughed about not deigning to belong to a club that would accept someone like him as a member, a truth as appropriate in love as it is in club membership. We laugh at the Marxist position because of its absurd contradictions: How is it possible that I should both wish to join a club, and yet lose that wish as soon as it comes true? How was it that I might have wished Chloe to love me, but have been irritated by her when she did so?

16.   Perhaps because the origins of a certain kind of love lie in an impulse to escape ourselves and our weaknesses by an alliance with the beautiful and noble. But if the loved ones love us back, we are forced to return to ourselves, and are hence reminded of the things that had driven us into love in the first place. Perhaps it was not love we wanted after all, perhaps it was simply someone in whom to believe, but how can we continue to believe in the beloved now that they believe in us?

17.   I wondered how Chloe could be justified in even thinking she could base her emotional life around a scoundrel like me. If she appeared to be a little in love, was this not simply because she had misunderstood me?

18.   Though from a position of unrequited love they long to see their love returned, Marxists unconsciously prefer that their dreams remain in the realm of fantasy. Why should others think any better of them than they of themselves? Only so long as the loved one believes the Marxist to be more or less nothing, can the Marxist continue to believe the loved one to be more or less everything. If Chloe had been lowered in my estimation because she had slept with me, it was because she had in the process caught a bad case of *I-infection*.

19.   I had often seen Marxism at work in others. At the age of sixteen, I was for a while in love with a fifteen-year-old girl, who was both captain of her school volleyball team, very beautiful, and a committed Marxist.

'If a man says he'll call me at nine,' she once told me over a glass of orange squash that I bought for her at the school cafeteria, 'and he does actually ring at nine, I'll refuse to take the call. After all, what's he so desperate for? The only guy I like is the one who'll keep me waiting, by nine thirty I'll do anything for him.'

I must at that age have had an intuitive understanding of her Marxism, for I remember efforts to seem uninterested in anything she said or did. My reward came with our first kiss a few weeks later, but though she was unquestionably beautiful (and as adept at the arts of love as she was at volleyball), the relationship did not last. It was too tiring to make a point of always calling late.

20.   A few years later, I was seeing another girl, who (like a good Marxist) believed that men should in some way defy her in order to earn her love. One morning, before going out for a walk with her in the park, I had put on an old and particularly off-putting electric-blue pullover.

'Well, one thing is for sure, I'm not going out with you looking like that,' exclaimed Sophie when she saw me coming down the stairs. 'You've got to be joking if you think I'll be seen with someone with that kind of jumper on.'

'Sophie, what does it matter what I'm wearing? We're only going for a walk in the park,' I replied, half-fearing she was serious.

'I don't care where we're going, I tell you, I'm not going to the park with you unless you change.'

But pig-headedness descended on me and I refused to do as Sophie wanted, arguing the case of the electric jumper with such force that a while later we headed for the Royal Hospital Gardens with the offending garment still in place. When we reached the gates of the park, Sophie, who had till then been in a mild sulk, suddenly broke the silence, took my arm, gave me a kiss, and said in words that perhaps provide us with an essence of Marxism, 'Don't worry, I'm not angry with you, I'm glad you kept the old horror on, *I would have thought you were so weak if you'd done what I told you.*'

21.   To be loved by someone is to realize how much they share the same needs that lie at the heart of our own attraction to them. Albert Camus suggested that we fall in love

with people because, from the outside, they look so *whole*, physically whole and emotionally 'together' – when subjectively, we feel dispersed and confused. We would not love if there were no lack within us, but we are offended by the discovery of a similar lack in the other. Expecting to find the answer, we find only the duplicate of our own problem.

22. A long, gloomy tradition in Western thought argues that love is in its essence an unreciprocated, Marxist emotion and that desire can only thrive on the impossibility of mutuality. According to this view, love is simply a direction, not a place, and burns itself out with the attainment of its goal, the possession (in bed or otherwise) of the loved one. The whole of troubadour poetry of twelfth-century Provence was based on coital delay, the poet repeating his plaints to a woman who repeatedly declined a desperate gentleman's offers. Centuries later, Montaigne declared that, 'In love, there is nothing but a frantic desire for what flees from us' – an idea echoed by Anatole France's maxim that, 'It is not customary to love what one has.' Stendhal believed that love could be brought about only on the basis of a fear of losing the loved one and Denis de Rougemont confirmed, 'The most serious obstruction is the one preferred above all. It is the one most suited to intensifying passion.' To listen to this view, lovers cannot do anything save oscillate between the twin poles of yearning for someone and longing to be rid of them.

23. There was a danger that Chloe and I would trap ourselves in just such a Marxist spiral. But a happier resolution

emerged. I returned home from the breakfast guilty, shame-faced, apologetic, and ready to do anything to win Chloe back. It wasn't easy. She hung up on me at first, then asked me whether I made a point of behaving like a 'small-time suburban punk' with women I had slept with. But after apologies, insults, laughter, and tears, Romeo and Juliet were to be seen together later that afternoon, mushily holding hands in the dark at a four-thirty screening of *Love and Death* at the National Film Theatre. Happy endings – for now at least.

24. There is usually a Marxist moment in every relation-ship, the moment when it becomes clear that love is reciprocated. The way it is resolved depends on the balance between self-love and self-hatred. If self-hatred gains the upper hand, then the one who has received love will declare that the beloved (on some excuse or other) is not good enough for them (not good enough by virtue of associating with no-goods). But if self-love gains the upper hand, both partners may accept that seeing their love reciprocated is not proof of how low the beloved is, but of how lovable they have themselves turned out to be.

7

False Notes

1. Long before we've had a chance to become truly familiar with our loved one, we may be filled with the curious sense that we know them already. It can seem as though we've met them somewhere before, in a previous life, perhaps, or in our dreams. In Plato's *Symposium*, Aristophanes accounts for this feeling of familiarity by claiming that the loved one was our long-lost 'other half' to whose body our own had originally been joined. In the beginning, all human beings were hermaphrodites with double backs and flanks, four hands and four legs and two faces turned in opposite directions on the same head. These hermaphrodites were so powerful and their pride so overweening that Zeus was forced to cut them in two, into a male and female half – and from that day, every man and woman has yearned nostalgically but confusedly to rejoin the part from which he or she was severed.

2. Chloe and I spent Christmas apart, but when we returned to London in the new year, we began spending all our time in each other's company. We led the typical romance of late-twentieth-century urban life, sandwiched between office hours and animated by such minor external events as walks

in the park, strolls through bookshops, and meals in restaurants. We found agreement on so many different issues, we hated and loved so many of the same things, that, after only a short time, it seemed churlish to deny that, despite an absence of clear separation marks, we must once have been two parts of the same body.

3. It was congruence that made life with Chloe so attractive. After unending irreconcilable differences in matters of the heart, I had at last found someone whose jokes I understood without the need of a dictionary, whose views seemed miraculously close to mine, whose loves and hates kept tandem with my own and with whom I repeatedly found myself saying, '*It's amazing, I was about to say/think/do/express the same thing . . .*'

4. Theorists of love have tended to be rightly suspicious of fusion, their scepticism stemming from the sense that it is easier to impute similarity than investigate difference. We base our fall into love upon insufficient material, and supplement our ignorance with desire. But, these theorists point out, time will show us that the skin separating our bodies is not just a physical boundary, but is representative of a deeper, psychological watershed we would be foolish to try and cross.

5. Therefore, in the mature account of love, we should never fall at first glance. We should reserve our leap until we have completed a clear-eyed investigation of the depths

and nature of the waters. Only after we have undertaken a thorough exchange of opinions on parenting, politics, art, science, and appropriate snacks for the kitchen should two people ever decide they are ready to love each other. In the mature account of love, it is only when we truly know our partners that love deserves the chance to grow. And yet in the perverse reality of love (love that is born precisely *before* we know) increased knowledge may be as much a hurdle as an inducement – for it may bring Utopia into dangerous conflict with reality.

6. I date the realization that, whatever enticing similarities we had identified between us, Chloe was perhaps not the person from whom Zeus's cruel stroke had severed me, to a moment somewhere in the middle of March when she introduced me to a new pair of her shoes. It was perhaps a pedantic matter over which to come to such a decision, but shoes are supreme symbols of aesthetic, and hence by extension psychological, compatibility. Certain areas and coverings of the body say more about a person than others: shoes suggest more than pullovers, thumbs more than elbows, underwear more than overcoats, ankles more than shoulders.

7. What was wrong with Chloe's shoes? Objectively speaking, nothing – but when did one ever fall in love *objectively*? She had bought them one Saturday morning in a shop on the King's Road, ready for a party we had been invited to that evening. I understood the blend of high- and low-heeled shoe that the designer had tried to fuse, the platformed sole rising

sharply up to a heel with the breadth of a flat shoe but the height of a stiletto. Then there was the high, faintly rococo collar, decorated with a bow and stars, and framed by a piece of chunky ribbon. The shoes were the apogee of fashion, they were well made, they were imaginative, and I detested them.

8. 'I know you're going to love them,' said Chloe, unfurling the purple tissue paper in which they had come, 'I'm going to wear them every day. Then again, they're so amazing, maybe I should just wrap them back up, leave them in their box, and never use them.'

'That's an interesting idea.'

'I could have bought the shop. They've got such great things there. You should have seen the boots they had.'

My mouth went dry. I felt a strange throbbing movement at the back of my neck. I couldn't conceive how Chloe had lost her heart to a deeply compromised piece of footwear. My idea of who she was, my Aristophanic certainty of her identity, had never included this sort of enthusiasm. Hurt and disturbed by the unexpected turn in our relationship, I asked myself, 'How could a woman who walks into my life (in sensible flat black shoes favoured by schoolgirls and nuns) and claims to love and understand me be drawn to such shoes?' Yet outwardly, I simply enquired (in what I trusted to be a remarkably innocent tone), 'Did you keep the receipt?'

9. It promptly seemed easier to love Chloe without knowing her. In one of his prose poems, Baudelaire describes how a man spends a day walking around Paris with a woman

he feels ready to fall in love with. They agree on so many things that by evening, he is convinced he has found a companion with whose soul his own may unite. Thirsty, they go to a glamorous new cafe on the corner of a boulevard, where the man notices the arrival of an impoverished, working-class family who have come to gaze through the plate-glass window of the cafe at the elegant guests, dazzling white walls, and gilded decor. The eyes of these poor on-lookers are full of wonder at the display of wealth and beauty inside, and their expression fills the narrator with pity and shame at his privileged position. He turns to look at his loved one in the hope of seeing his embarrassment and emotion reflected in her eyes. But the woman with whose soul his own was prepared to unite has a different agenda. She snaps that these wretches with their wide, gaping eyes are unbearable to her, she wonders what on earth they want and asks him to tell the owner to have them moved on straightaway. Does not every love story have these moments? A search for eyes that will reflect one's thoughts and that ends up with a (tragi-comic) divergence – be it over the class struggle or a pair of shoes.

10. Perhaps the easiest people to fall in love with are those about whom we know nothing. Romances are never as pure as those we imagine during long train journeys, as we secretly contemplate a beautiful person who is gazing out of the window – a perfect love story interrupted only when the beloved looks back into the carriage and starts up a dull conversation about the excessive price of the on-board

sandwiches with a neighbour or blows her nose aggressively into a handkerchief.

11. The dismay that greater acquaintance with the beloved can bring is comparable to composing a symphony in one's head and then hearing it played in a concert hall by a full orchestra. Though we are impressed to find so many of our ideas confirmed in performance, we cannot help but notice details that are not quite as we had intended them to be. Is one of the violinists not a little off key? Is the flute not a little late coming in? Is the percussion not a little loud? People we love at first sight are as free from conflicting tastes in shoes or literature as the unrehearsed symphony is free from off-key violins or late flutes. But as soon as the fantasy is played out, the angelic beings who floated through consciousness reveal themselves as material beings, laden with their own mental and physical history.

12. Chloe's shoes were only one of a number of false notes that came to light in the early period of the relationship. Living day to day with her was like acclimatizing myself to a foreign country, and therefore feeling prey to occasional xenophobia at departures from my own traditions and expectations.

13. Threatening differences did not collect at the major points (nationality, gender, class, occupation), but rather at small junctures of taste and opinion. Why did Chloe insist on leaving the pasta to boil for a fatal extra few minutes?

Why was I so attached to my current pair of glasses? Why did she have to do her gym exercises in the bedroom every morning? Why did I always need eight hours' sleep? Why did she not have more time for opera? Why did I not have more time for Joni Mitchell? Why did she hate seafood so much? How could one explain my resistance to flowers and gardening? Or hers to trips on water? How come she liked to keep her options open about God (*'at least till the first cancer'*)? But why was I so closed on the matter?

14. Anthropologists tell us that the group always comes before the individual, that to understand the latter one must pass through the former, be it nation, tribe, clan, or family. Chloe had no great fondness for her family, but when her parents invited us to spend Sunday with them at their home near Marlborough, in a spirit of scientific enquiry I urged her to take up the offer.

15. Everything about Gnarled Oak Cottage was a sign that Chloe had been born in one world, one galaxy almost, and I another. The living room was decorated in faux-Chippendale furniture, the carpet was a stained reddish brown, dusty bookcases with volumes of Trollope and Stubbs-esque paintings lined the walls, three salival dogs were running in and out between the living room and the garden, and corpulent cobwebbed plants sagged in every corner. Chloe's mother wore a thick purple pullover with holes in it, a flowery baggy skirt, and long grey hair scraped back without design. One

half expected to find bits of straw on her, an aura of rural non-
chalance reinforced by her repeated forgettings of my name
(and her creative approach to finding me another). I thought
of the difference between Chloe's mother and my own, the
contrasting introductions to the world that these two women
had performed. However much Chloe had run away from all
of this, to the big city, to her own values and friends, the
family still represented a genetic and historical tradition to
which she was indebted. I noticed a crossover between the
generations: the mother preparing potatoes in the same way
as Chloe, crushing a little garlic into the butter and grinding sea salt over them, or sharing her daughter's enthusiasm
for painting, or taste in Sunday papers. The father was a keen
rambler, and Chloe loved walking too, often dragging me on
weekends for a brisk tour of Hampstead Heath, proclaiming
the benefits of fresh air in a way that her father had perhaps
once done.

16.   It was all so strange and new. The house in which she
had grown up evoked a whole past on which I had missed out,
and which I would have to take on board in order to understand her. The meal was largely spent on a question–answer
volley between Chloe and her parents on various aspects of
family folklore: Had the insurance paid for Granny's hospital
bills? Was the water tank mended? Had Carolyn heard from
the estate agency yet? Was it true Lucy was going to study
in the States? Had anyone read Aunt Sarah's novel? Was
Henry really going to marry Jemima? (All these characters

who had entered Chloe's life long before I had – and might, with the tenacity of everything familial, still be there when I was gone.)

17. It was intriguing to see how different the parents' perception of Chloe could be from my own. Whereas I had known her to be both accommodating and generous, at home she was known to be bossy and demanding. As a child she had been thought of as miniature autocrat whom the parents had nicknamed Miss Pompadosso after the heroine of a children's book. Whereas I had known Chloe to be level-headed about money and her career, the father remarked that his daughter 'did not understand the first thing about how things work in the real world', while the mother joked about her 'bullying all her boyfriends into submission'. I was forced to add to my understanding of Chloe a whole section that had unfolded prior to my arrival, my vision of her colliding with that imposed by the initial family narrative.

18. In the afternoon, Chloe showed me around the house. She took me into the room at the top of the stairs into which she'd been afraid to go as a child, because her uncle had once told her a ghost lived inside the piano. We looked into her old bedroom that her mother now used as a studio, and she pointed out a hatch that she had used to get into the attic in order to escape with her elephant Guppy whenever she'd been miserable. We took a walk in the garden, past a still-bruised tree at the bottom of a slope into which the family car had ploughed when she had once dared her brother to release

the handbrake. She showed me the neighbours' house, whose
blackberry bushes she had picked clean in the summers, and
whose former owner's son she had kissed on the way back
from school. He had since died, added Chloe with curious
indifference, 'in an incident with a corn-thresher'.

19. Later in the afternoon, I took a walk in the garden with
her father, a donnish man to whom thirty years of marriage
had imparted some distinctive views on the subject.

'I know my daughter and you are fond of one another.
I'm no expert on love, but I'll tell you something. In the
end, I've found that it doesn't really matter who you marry.
If you like them at the beginning, you probably won't like
them at the end. And if you start off hating them, there's
always the chance you'll end up thinking they're all right.'

20. On the train back to London that evening, I felt
exhausted, weary at all the differences between Chloe's
early world and mine. While the stories and settings of
her past had enchanted me, they had also proved terrifying
and bizarre, all these years and habits before I had known
her, but that were as much a part of who she was as the
shape of her nose or the colour of her eyes. I felt a primitive
nostalgia for familiar surroundings, recognizing the disruption that every relationship entails – a whole new person to
learn about, to suggest myself to, to acclimatize myself to.
It was perhaps a moment of fear at the thought of all the
differences I would find in Chloe, all the times she would
be one thing, and I another, when our world views would be

incapable of alignment. Staring out of the window at the Wiltshire countryside, I had a lost child's longing for someone I could already wholly understand, the eccentricities of whose house, parents, and history I had already tamed.

8

Love or Liberalism

1. If I can return for a moment to Chloe's shoes, it might be worth mentioning that their inauguration did not end with my negative yet privately formulated analysis of their virtues. I confess that it ended in the second greatest argument of our relationship, in tears, insults, shouting, and the right shoe crashing through a pane of glass onto the pavement of Denbigh Street. The sheer melodramatic intensity of the event aside, the matter sustains philosophical interest because it symbolizes a choice as radical in the personal sphere as in the political: a choice between *love* and *liberalism*.

2. The choice has often been missed in an optimistic equation of the two terms, with the former considered a handmaiden of the latter. But if the terms have been linked, it is always in an implausible marriage, for it seems impossible to talk of love *and* letting live, and if we are left to live, we are not usually loved. We may well ask why the viciousness witnessed between lovers would not be tolerated anywhere outside conditions of open enmity. Then, to build bridges between shoes and nations, we may ask why

countries that have no language of community or citizen-
ship usually leave their members isolated but unmolested
and yet why countries that talk most of love, kinship, and
brotherhood routinely end up slaughtering great swathes of
their populations.

3. 'How do you mean, did I *keep the receipt?*' shouted Chloe.
'I just mean if things go wrong with them.'
'They're not televisions.'
'I don't know, the heel might get stuck between two
paving stones while you're stepping out of a gondola. Or
you might suddenly decide you hated them.'
'Why not just tell me *you* hate them?'
'I don't hate them. (Pause.) I do hate them.'
'You're just jealous.'
'I've always wanted to look like a pelican.'
'And a bastard.'
'I'm sorry, but I really don't think they're suitable for the
party tonight.'
'Why do you have to spoil everything?'
'Because I care for you. *Someone* has to let you know the
truth.'
'Gemma said she liked them. And Leslie would defi-
nitely like them. And I can't imagine Abigail having a
problem with them either. So what's wrong with you?'
'Your girlfriends don't love you. Not in the proper way.
Not in the way that means you have to break bad news to
someone even if it pains you terribly.'
'You're not upset.'

'I am.'

'You deserve to be.'

4. The reader can be spared the full melodrama, it suffices to say that moments later, the tempest that had been brewing reached a climax, Chloe took off one of the offensive shoes, supposedly so as to let me look at it, but more realistically, to murder me with it, I chose to duck the incoming projectile, it crashed through the window behind me and fell down to the street, where it impaled itself in the rubbish area in the remains of a neighbour's chicken madras.

5. Our argument was peppered with the paradoxes of love and liberalism. What did it really matter what Chloe's shoes were like? There were so many other wonderful sides to her, was it not spoiling the game to arrest my gaze on this detail? Why could I not have politely lied to her as I might have done to a friend? My only excuse lay in the claim that I loved her, that she was my ideal – save for the shoes – and that I therefore had to point out this blemish, something I would never have done with a friend whose departures from my ideal would have been too numerous to begin with, a friendship in which the concept of an ideal would never even have entered into my thinking. *Because I loved her, I told her* – therein lay my sole defence.

6. In our more expansive moments, we imagine romantic love to be akin to Christian love, an uncritical, expansive emotion that declares *I will love you for everything that you are,*

a love that has no conditions, that draws no boundaries, that adores every last shoe, that is the embodiment of acceptance. But the arguments that hound lovers are a reminder that Christian love is not prone to survive a move into the bedroom. Its message seems more suited to the universal than the particular, to the love of all men for all women, to the love of two neighbours who will not hear each other snoring.

7.   Though it was not always a matter for glaziers, illiberalism was never one sided. There were a thousand things about me that drove Chloe to distraction: Why was I so bored by the theatre? Why did I insist on wearing a coat that looked a century old? Why did I always knock the duvet off the bed in my sleep? Why did I think Saul Bellow was such a great writer? Why had I not yet learnt how to park a car without leaving most of the wheel on the pavement? Why did I constantly put my feet on the pillows? These were the ingredients of the domestic gulag, the daily attempts to tug each other closer to our ideals.

8.   And what excuse was there for this? Nothing but the old line that parents and politicians will use before taking out their scalpels: *I care about you, therefore I will upset you, I have honoured you with a vision of how you should be, therefore I will hurt you.*

9.   Chloe and I would never have been as brutal to our friends as we were to one another. But we equated intimacy with a form of ownership and licence. We may have been

kind, yet we were no longer polite. When we started arguing one night about the films of Eric Rohmer (she hated
them, I loved them), we forgot there was a chance Rohmer's
films could be both good and bad depending on who was
watching them. She degenerated into calling me 'a stuffy
over-intellectual turd', I reciprocated by judging her 'a
degenerate product of modern capitalism' (proving her
accusation in the process).

10.   Politics seems an incongruous field to link to love, but
can we not read, in the bloodstained histories of the French,
Fascist, or Communist revolutions, something of the same
coercive structure, the same impatience with diverging
views fuelled by passionate ideals? Amorous politics begins
its infamous history with the French Revolution, when it was
first proposed (with all the choice of a rape) that the state
would not just govern but also *love* its citizens, who would
respond likewise or face the guillotine. The beginning of revolutions is psychologically strikingly akin to that of certain
relationships: the stress on unity, the sense of omnipotence,
the desire to eliminate secrets (with the fear of the opposite
soon leading to lover's paranoia and the creation of a secret
police).

11.   But if the beginnings of love and amorous politics are
equally rosy, then the ends are often equally bloody. We're
familiar with political love that ends in tyranny, where a
ruler's firm conviction that he has the true interests of his
nation at heart ends up lending him the confidence to

murder without qualms (and 'for their own good') all who disagree with him. Romantic lovers are similarly inclined to vent their frustration on dissenters and heretics.

12. A few days after the shoe incident, I went to the newsagent to pick up a paper and a carton of milk. Mr Paul told me he'd just run out of the semi-skimmed variety, but that if I could wait a moment, he'd get another crate in from the storeroom. Watching him walk out towards the back of the shop, I noticed that Mr Paul was wearing a pair of thick grey socks and brown leather sandals. They were awe-inspiringly ugly, but curiously enough, wholly inoffensive. Why could I not remain similarly composed in the face of Chloe's shoes? Why could I not enjoy the same cordiality with the woman I loved as with the newsagent who sold me my daily rations?

13. The wish to replace the butcher–butchered relationship with a newsagent–customer one has long dominated political thinking. Why could rulers not act politely towards their citizens, tolerating sandals, dissent, and divergence? The answer from liberal thinkers is that cordiality can arise only once rulers give up talk of governing for the love of their citizens, and concentrate instead on ensuring sensible, minimal governance. Liberal politics finds its greatest apologist in John Stuart Mill, who in 1859 published a classic defence of loveless liberalism, *On Liberty*, a ringing plea that citizens should be left alone by governments, however well meaning they were, and not be told how to lead their personal lives,

what gods to worship or books to read. Mill argued that though kingdoms and tyrannies felt themselves entitled to hold 'a deep interest in the whole bodily and mental discipline of every one of its citizens', the modern state should as far as possible stand back and let people govern themselves. Like a harassed partner in a relationship who begs simply to be given space, Mill ventured:

> The only freedom which deserves the name is that of pursuing our own good, in our own way, so long as we do not attempt to deprive others of theirs, or impede their efforts to obtain it . . . The only purpose for which power can be rightfully exercised over any member of a civilized society against his will is to prevent harm to others. His own good, either physical or moral, is not sufficient warrant.*

14. The wisdom of Mill's thesis is such that one might want to see it applied to relationships as much as to governments. However, on reflection, applied to the former, it seems to lose much of its appeal. It evokes certain marriages, where love has evaporated long ago, where couples sleep in separate bedrooms, exchanging the occasional word when they meet in the kitchen before work, where both partners have long ago given up hope of mutual understanding, settling instead for a tepid friendship based on controlled misunderstanding, politeness while they get through the evening's shepherd's pie, 3 a.m. bitterness at the emotional failure that surrounds them.

---

* *On Liberty*, John Stuart Mill (Cambridge University Press, 1989).

15. We seem to be thrown back on a choice between love and liberalism. The sandals of the newsagent didn't annoy me because I didn't care for him, I wished to get my paper and milk and leave. I didn't wish to cry on his shoulder or bare my soul, so his footwear remained unobtrusive. But had I fallen in love with Mr Paul, could I really have continued to face his sandals with equanimity, or would there not have come a point when (out of love) I would have cleared my throat and suggested an alternative?

16. If my relationship with Chloe never reached the levels of the Terror, it was perhaps because she and I were able to temper the choice between love and liberalism with an ingredient that too few relationships and even fewer amorous politicians (Lenin, Pol Pot, Robespierre) have ever possessed, an ingredient that might just (were there enough of it to go around) save both states and couples from intolerance: a sense of humour.

17. It seems significant that revolutionaries share with lovers a tendency towards terrifying earnestness. It is as hard to imagine cracking a joke with Stalin as with Young Werther. Both of them seem desperately, though differently, intense. With the inability to laugh comes an inability to acknowledge the contradictions inherent in every society and relationship, the multiplicity and clash of desires, the need to accept that one's partner will never learn how to park a car, or wash out a bath or give up a taste for Joni Mitchell – but that one cares for them rather a lot nevertheless.

18. If Chloe and I overcame certain of our differences, it was because we had the will to make jokes of the impasses we found in each other's characters. I could not stop hating Chloe's shoes, she continued to like them (I was sent down to pick the left one up and give it a clean), but we at least found room to turn the incident into a joke. By threatening to 'defenestrate' ourselves whenever arguments became heated, we were always sure to draw a laugh and neutralize a frustration. My driving techniques could not be improved, but they earned me the name 'Alain Prost', Chloe's attempts at martyrdom I found wearing, but less so when I could respond to them by calling her 'Joan of Arc'. Humour meant there was no need for a direct confrontation, we could glide over an irritant, winking at it obliquely, making a criticism without needing to spell it out.

19. It may be a sign that two people have stopped loving one another (or at least stopped wishing to make the effort that constitutes ninety per cent of love) when they are no longer able to spin differences into jokes. Humour lined the walls of irritation between our ideals and the reality: behind every joke, there was a warning of difference, of disappointment even, but it was a difference that had been defused – and could therefore be passed over without the need for a pogrom.

9

Beauty

1. Does beauty give birth to love or does love give birth to beauty? Did I love Chloe because she was beautiful or was she beautiful because I loved her? Surrounded by an infinite number of people, we may ask (staring at our lover while they talk on the phone or lie opposite us in the bath) why our desire has chosen to settle on this particular face, this particular mouth or nose or ear, why this curve of the neck or dimple in the cheek has come to answer so precisely to our criterion of perfection? Every one of our lovers offers different solutions to the problem of beauty, and yet succeeds in redefining our notions of attractiveness in a way that is as original and as idiosyncratic as the landscape of their face.

2. If Marsilio Ficino (1433–99) defined love as 'the desire for beauty', in what ways did Chloe fulfil this desire? To listen to Chloe, in no way whatever. No amount of reassurance could persuade her that she was anything but loathsome. She insisted on finding her nose too small, her mouth too wide, her chin uninteresting, her ears too round, her eyes not green enough, her hair not wavy enough, her breasts too small, her feet too large, her hands too wide, and

her wrists too narrow. She would gaze longingly at the faces in the pages of *Elle* and *Vogue* and declare that the concept of a just God was – in the light of her physical appearance – simply an incoherence.

3. Chloe believed that beauty could be measured according to an objective standard, one she had simply failed to reach. Without acknowledging it as such, she was resolutely attached to a Platonic concept of beauty, an aesthetic she shared with the world's fashion magazines and which fuelled a daily sense of self-loathing in front of the mirror. According to Plato and the editor of *Vogue*, there exists such a thing as an ideal form of beauty, made up of a balanced relation between parts, and which earthly bodies will approximate to a greater or a lesser degree. There is a mathematical basis for beauty, Plato suggested, so that the face on the front cover of a magazine is necessarily rather than coincidentally pleasing.

4. Whatever mathematical errors there were in her face, Chloe found the rest of her body even more unbalanced. Whereas I loved to watch soapy water running over her stomach and legs in the shower, whenever she looked at herself in the mirror she would invariably declare that something was 'lopsided' – though quite what I never discovered. Leon Battista Alberti (1409–72) might have known better, for he believed that any beautiful body had fixed proportions which he spelt out mathematically after dividing the body of a beautiful Italian girl into six hundred units, then

working out the distances from section to section. Summing up his results in his book *On Sculpture*, Alberti defined beauty as 'a Harmony of all the Parts, in whatsoever Subject it appears, fitted together with such proportion and connection, that nothing could be added, diminished or altered, but for the worse'. But according to Chloe, however, almost anything about her body could have been added, diminished, or altered without spoiling anything that nature had not already devastated.

5. Clearly Plato and Leon Battista Alberti had neglected something in their aesthetic theories, for I found Chloe excessively beautiful. Did I like her green eyes, her dark hair, her full mouth? I hesitate to try and pin down her appeal. Discussions of physical beauty have some of the futility of debates between art historians attempting to justify the relative merits of different artists. A Van Gogh or a Gauguin? One might try to redescribe the work in language ('the lyrical intelligence of Gauguin's South Sea skies . . .' next to 'the Wagnerian depth of Van Gogh's blues . . .') or else to elucidate technique or materials ('the Expressionist feel of Van Gogh's later years . . .' 'Gauguin's Cézanne-like linearity . . .'). But what would all this do to explain why one painting grips us by the collar and another leaves us cold? The language of the eye stubbornly resists translation into the language of words.

6. It was not beauty that I could hope to describe, only my personal response to Chloe's appearance. I could simply point

out where my desire had happened to settle, while allowing the possibility that others would locate comparable perfection in quite other beings. In so doing, I was forced to reject the Platonic idea of an objective criterion of beauty, siding instead with Kant's view, as expressed in his *Critique of Judgement*, that aesthetic judgements are ones 'whose determining ground can be none other than subjective'.

7. The way I looked at Chloe could have been compared to the famous Müller–Lyer illusion, where two lines of identical length will appear to be of different sizes according to the nature of the arrows attached at their ends. The loving way that I gazed at Chloe functioned like a pair of outward arrows, which give an ordinary line a semblance of length it might not objectively deserve.

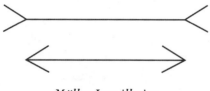

Müller–Lyer illusion

8. A definition of beauty that more accurately summed up my feelings for Chloe was delivered by Stendhal. 'Beauty is the promise of happiness,' he wrote, pointing to the way that Chloe's face alluded to qualities that I identified with a good life: there was humour in her nose, her freckles spoke of innocence, and her teeth suggested a casual, cheeky disregard for convention. I did not see the gap between her two front teeth

as an offensive deviation from an ideal arrangement, but as an indicator of psychological virtue.

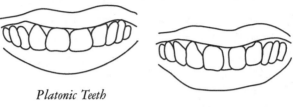

Platonic Teeth

Stendhalian Teeth

9.   I took pride in finding Chloe more beautiful than a Platonist would have done. The most interesting faces generally oscillate between charm and crookedness. There is a tyranny about perfection, a certain tedium even, something that asserts itself with all the dogmatism of a scientific formula. The more tempting kind of beauty has only a few angles from which it may be seen, and then not in all lights and at all times. It flirts dangerously with ugliness, it takes risks with itself, it does not side comfortably with mathematical rules of proportion, it draws its appeal from precisely those details that also lend themselves to ugliness. As Proust once said, classically beautiful women should be left to men without imagination.

10.   My imagination enjoyed playing in the space between Chloe's teeth. Her beauty was fractured enough that it could support creative rearrangements. In its ambiguity, her face could have been compared to Wittgenstein's duck-rabbit, where both a duck and a rabbit seem contained in the same

image. Much depends on the attitude of the viewer: if the imagination is looking for a duck, it will find one, if it is looking for a rabbit, it will appear instead. What counts is the predisposition of the viewer. It was of course love that was generously predisposing me. The editor of *Vogue* might have had difficulty including photos of Chloe in an issue, but this was only a confirmation of the uniqueness that I had managed to find in my girlfriend. I had animated her face with her soul.

Wittgenstein's Duck-Rabbit

11. The danger with the kind of beauty that does not look like a Greek statue is that its precariousness places much emphasis on the viewer. Once the imagination decides to remove itself from the gap in the teeth, is it not time for a good orthodontist? Once we locate beauty in the eye of the beholder, what will happen when the beholder looks elsewhere? But perhaps that was all part of Chloe's appeal. A subjective theory of beauty makes the observer wonderfully indispensable.

10

Speaking Love

1. In the middle of May, Chloe celebrated her twenty-fourth birthday. She had for a long time been dropping hints about a red cashmere pullover in the window of a shop in Piccadilly, so the day before the celebration, I bought it on my way back from work, and at home, wrapped it in blue paper with a pink bow. But in the course of preparing a card, I suddenly realized that I had never told Chloe that I loved her.

2. A declaration would perhaps not have been unexpected, yet the fact that it had never been made was significant. Pullovers may be a sign of love between a man and a woman, but we had yet to translate our feelings into language. It was as though the core of our relationship, configured around the word *love*, was somehow unmentionable, either too evident or too significant to be uttered.

3. It was simple to understand why Chloe had never said anything. She was suspicious of words. *'One can talk problems into existence,'* she had once said, and just as problems could

come from words, so good things could be destroyed by them. I remembered her telling me that, when she was twelve, her parents had sent her on a camping holiday. There she had fallen in love with a boy her age, and after much blushing and hesitation, they had ended up taking a walk around a lake. By a shaded bank, the boy had asked her to sit down, and after a moment, had taken her damp hand in his. It was the first time a boy had held her hand. She had been so elated, she had felt free to tell him, with all the earnestness of a twelve-year-old, that he was 'the best thing that had ever happened to her'. The next day, she discovered that her words had spread all over the camp. A group of girls chanted mockingly 'the best thing that ever happened to me' when she came into the dining hall, her honest declaration replayed in a mockery of her vulnerability. She had experienced a betrayal at the hands of language, the way intimate words may be converted to a common currency, and had since hidden behind a veil of practicality and irony.

4. With her customary resistance to the rose-tinted, Chloe would therefore probably have shrugged off a declaration with a joke, not because she did not want to hear, but because any formulation would have seemed dangerously close both to complete cliché and total nakedness. It was not that Chloe was unsentimental, she was just too discreet with her emotions to speak about them in the worn, social language of the romantic. Though her feelings may have been directed towards me, in a curious sense, *they were not for me to know.*

5. My pen was still hesitating over the card (a giraffe was blowing out candles on a heart-shaped cake). Whatever her resistance and my qualms, I felt that the occasion of her birthday called for a linguistic confirmation of the bond between us. I tried to imagine what she would make of the words I might hand her, I pictured her thinking about them on the way to work or in the bath, pleased but reluctant even to savour her own satisfaction.

6. Yet the difficulty of a declaration of love opens up quasi-philosophical concerns about language. If I told Chloe that I had a stomach ache or a garden full of daffodils, I could count on her to understand. Naturally, my image of a be-daffodiled garden might slightly differ from hers, but there would be reasonable parity between the two images. Words would operate as reliable messengers of meaning. But the card I was now trying to write had no such guarantees attached to it. The words were the most ambiguous in the language, because the things they referred to so sorely lacked stable meaning. Certainly travellers had returned from the heart and tried to represent what they had seen, but love was in the end like a species of rare coloured butterfly, often sighted, but never conclusively identified.

7. The thought was a lonely one: of the error one may find over a single word, an argument not for linguistic pedants, but of desperate importance to lovers who need to make themselves understood. Chloe and I could both speak of being in love, and yet this love might mean significantly

different things within each of us. We had often read the same books at night in the same bed, and later realized that they had touched us in different places: that they had been different books for each of us. Might the same divergence not occur over a single love-line? I felt like a dandelion releasing hundreds of spores into the air – and not knowing if any of them would get through.

8. The whole language of love had been corrupted by overuse. When I listened to the radio in the car, my love fed effortlessly off the love songs that happened to be playing, for example, off the passion of a black American female singer, whose accent I took on (I was on an empty motorway) while Chloe became the lady's 'baby'.

> *Wouldn't it be nice*
> *To hold you in my arms*
> *And love you, baby?*
> *To hold you in my arms*
> *Oh yeah and I say, I do, I say I love you baby?*

9. How much of what I thought I felt for Chloe had been influenced by songs like these? Was my sense of being in love not just the result of living in a particular cultural epoch? Was it not society, rather than any authentic urge, that was motivating me to pride myself on romantic love? In previous cultures and ages, would I not have been taught to ignore my feelings for Chloe in the way I was now taught to ignore (more or less) the impulse to wear stockings or to respond to insult with a challenge to a duel?

'*Some people would never have fallen in love if they had never heard of love,*' aphorized La Rochefoucauld, and does not history prove him right? I was due to take Chloe to a Chinese restaurant in Camden, but declarations of love might have seemed more appropriate elsewhere given the scant regard traditionally given to love in Chinese culture. According to the psychological anthropologist L. K. Hsu, whereas Western cultures are 'individual-centred' and place great emphasis on emotions, in contrast, Chinese culture is 'situation-centred' and concentrates on groups rather than couples and their love (though the manager of the Lao Tzu was nevertheless delighted to take my booking). Love is never a given, it is constructed and defined by different societies. In at least one society, the Manu of New Guinea, there is not even a word for love. In other cultures, love exists, but is given distinctive forms. Ancient Egyptian love poetry had no interest in the emotions of shame, guilt, or ambivalence. The Greeks thought nothing of homo-sexuality, Christianity proscribed the body, the Troubadours equated love with unrequited passion, the Romantics made love into a religion, and the perhaps not-very-happily married S. M. Greenfield, in an article in the *Sociological Quarterly* which I had picked up at the dentist (I don't know what it was doing there either), wrote that love is today kept alive by modern capitalism only in order to:

> . . . motivate individuals – where there is no other means
> of motivating them – to occupy the positions husband-
> father and wife-mother and form nuclear families that are
> essential not only for reproduction and socialization but

also to maintain the existing arrangements for distributing and consuming goods and services and, in general,
to keep the social system in proper working order and
thus maintain it as a going concern.

10. The sickness, nausea, and longing that I had at times
felt at the thought of Chloe might in some societies have
been identified as signs of a religious experience. When
St Teresa of Avila (1515–82), founder of the Discalced
Carmelite Order, had a visit from an angel, she described
an encounter which it would take a particularly open contemporary mind not to identify with an orgasm:

> The angel was very beautiful, his face was so aflame that
> he appeared to be one of the highest types of angels who
> seem to be all afire . . . In his hands I saw a golden spear
> and at the end of the iron tip I seemed to see a point of
> fire. With this he seemed to pierce my heart several times
> so that it penetrated my entrails . . . The pain was so sharp
> that it made me utter several moans; and so excessive was
> the sweetness caused me by this intense pain that one can
> never wish to lose it, nor will one's soul be content with
> anything less than God.

11. In the end, I decided that a card with a giraffe might
not be the best place to articulate my feelings – and that
I should wait till dinner. At around eight, I drove to
Chloe's apartment to pick her up and give her the present.
She was delighted to find that I had heard her hints about
the Piccadilly window, the only regret (tactfully delivered

a few days later) was that it had been the blue and not the red pullover she'd really been pointing to (though receipts gave us a second chance, after I had tried to but been desisted from throwing myself out of the window).

12.   The restaurant could not have been more romantic. All around us in the Lao Tzu, couples much like ourselves (though our subjective sense of uniqueness did not allow us to think so) were holding hands, drinking wine, and fumbling with chopsticks (a neighbour's cashew nut came at one point to rest on Chloe's lap).

'God, I feel better, I must have been starving. I've been so depressed all day,' said Chloe.

'Why?'

'Because I have this thing about birthdays, they always remind me of death and forced jollity. But actually, I think this one's turning out to be not so bad in the end. In fact, it's pretty all right, thanks to a little help from my friend.'

She looked up at me and smiled.

'You know where I was this time last year?' she asked.

'No, where?'

'Being taken out for dinner by my horrible aunt. It was awful, I kept having to go to the bathroom to cry, I was so upset that it was my birthday and the only person who'd invited me out was my aunt with this irritating stutter who couldn't stop telling me she didn't understand how a nice girl like me didn't have a man in her life. So it's probably no bad thing I ran into you . . .'

13. She really was adorable (thought the lover, a most unreliable witness in such matters). But how could I tell her so in a way that would suggest the distinctive nature of my attraction? Words like *love* or *devotion* or *infatuation* were exhausted by the weight of successive love stories, by the layers imposed on them through the uses of others. At the moment when I most wanted language to be original, personal, and completely private, I came up against the irrevocably public nature of emotional communication.

14. The restaurant was of no help, for its romantic setting made love too conspicuous, hence insincere. There was a recording of Chopin's *Nocturnes* over the loudspeakers and a heart-shaped candle on the table. We overheard a man at the next table (perhaps a Darwinist) joking it should have been a penis. There seemed to be no way to transport *love* in the word L-O-V-E without at the same time throwing the most banal associations into the basket. The word was too rich in foreign history: everything from the Troubadours to *Casablanca* had cashed in on the letters. Was it not my duty to be the author of my own feelings? Would I not have to fashion a declaration with a uniqueness to match Chloe's? I felt disconcertingly aware of the mundanity of our situation: *a man and a woman, lovers, celebrating a birthday in a Chinese restaurant, one night in the Western world, somewhere towards the end of the twentieth century.* No, my meaning could never make the journey in L-O-V-E. It would have to seek alternative transportation.

15.   Then I noticed a small plate of complimentary marsh-
mallows near Chloe's elbow and it suddenly seemed clear
that I didn't *love* Chloe so much as *marshmallow* her. What
it was about a marshmallow that should suddenly have
accorded so perfectly with my feelings towards her I will
never know, but the word seemed to capture the essence of
my amorous state with an accuracy that the word love, weary
with overuse, simply could not aspire to. Even more inex-
plicably, when I took Chloe's hand and told her that I had
something very important to tell her, that I *marshmallowed*
her, she seemed to understand perfectly, answering it was the
sweetest thing anyone had ever told her.

16.   From then on, love was, for Chloe and me at least, no
longer simply *love*, it was a sugary, puffy object a few mil-
limetres in diameter that melts deliciously in the mouth.

11

What Do You See in Her?

1.   Summer flew in with the first week of June, making a Mediterranean city of London, drawing people from their homes and offices into the parks and squares. The heat coincided with the arrival of a new colleague at work, an American architect, who had been hired to spend six months working with us on an office complex near Waterloo.

2.   'They told me it rained every day in London – and look at this!' remarked Will as we sat one lunchtime in a restaurant in Covent Garden. 'Incredible, and I brought only pullovers.'

'Don't worry, Will, they have T-shirts here too.'

I had met William Knott five years before, when we had both spent a year together on scholarships at Yale. He was immensely tall, with the perpetual tan, intrepid smile, and rugged face of an explorer but the hands of a pianist. Since finishing his studies at Berkeley, he had developed a successful career on the West Coast, where he was considered one of the most thoughtful practitioners of his generation. The *Architects' Journal* had described him, with little concern for biological reality, as 'the illegitimate love-child of Mies van der Rohe and Geoffrey Bawa' and even the normally reserved *Architectural Review* had commended him on his use of concrete.

3. 'So tell me, are you seeing anyone?' asked Will as we began our coffee. 'You're not still with what's her name, that . . . ?'

'No, no, that finished long ago. I'm involved in something serious now.'

'Great, tell me about it.'

'Well, you must come over for dinner and meet her.'

'I'd love to. Tell me more.'

'She's called Chloe, she's twenty-four, she's a graphic designer. She's intelligent, beautiful, very funny . . .'

'It sounds terrific.'

'How about you?'

'Nothing to say really, I was dating this girl from UCLA, but you know, we were getting in each other's head-space, so we sort of both pulled the rip-cord. We weren't ready to ride the big one together, so . . . But tell me more about this Chloe, what is it you see in her?'

4. *What did I see in her?* The question came back to me later that evening in the middle of Safeway, watching Chloe at the till, enraptured by the way she went about packing the groceries into a plastic bag. The charm I detected in these trivial gestures revealed a readiness to accept almost anything as incontestable proof that she was perfect. *What did I see in her?* Almost everything.

5. For a moment, I fantasized I might transform myself into a carton of yogurt so as to undergo the same process of being gently and thoughtfully accommodated by her into a shopping bag between a tin of tuna and a bottle of olive oil. It was only the incongruously unsentimental atmosphere of the supermarket ('Liver Promotion Week') that alerted me to how far I might have been sliding into romantic pathology.

6. On the way back to the car, I complimented Chloe on the adorable way she had gone about the business of doing the grocery shopping.

'Don't be so silly,' she replied. 'Can you open the boot, the keys are in my bag.'

7. It is easy enough to find charm in a pair of eyes or the contours of a well-shaped mouth. How much harder to detect it in the movements of a woman's hand across a supermarket checkout. Chloe's gestures were like the tips of an iceberg, an indication of what lay submerged. Did it not require a lover to discern their true value, a value that would naturally seem meaningless to someone less curious, less in love?

8. Yet I remained pensive on the drive home through the evening rush hour. My love began to question itself. What did it mean if things I considered charming about Chloe, she considered incidental or irrelevant to her true self? Was I reading things into Chloe that simply did not belong to her? I looked at the slope of her shoulders and the way that a

strand of her hair was trapped in the car headrest. She turned towards me and smiled, so for an instant I saw the gap in between her two front teeth. How much of my sensitive, soulful lover lay in my fellow passenger?

9.   Love reveals its insanity by its refusal to acknowledge the inherent *normality* of the loved one. Hence the boredom of lovers for those standing on the sidelines. What do they see in the beloved save simply another human being? I had often tried to share my enthusiasm for Chloe with friends, with whom in the past I had found much common ground over films, books, and politics, but who now looked at me with the secular puzzlement of atheists faced with messianic fervour. After the tenth time of telling friends these stories of Chloe at the dry cleaner or Chloe and me at the cinema, or Chloe and me buying a takeaway, these stories with no plot and less action, just the central character standing in the centre of an almost motionless tale, I was forced to acknowledge that love was a lonely pursuit.

10.   There was of course nothing inherently lovable about Chloe's way of packing the groceries, love was merely something I had decided to ascribe to her gesture, a gesture that might have been interpreted very differently by others in line with us at Safeway. A person is never good or bad per se, which means that loving or hating them necessarily has at its basis a subjective, and perhaps illusionistic, element. I was reminded of the way that Will's question had made the distinction between qualities that belonged to a person and

those ascribed to them by their lover. He had carefully asked me not *who* Chloe was, but more accurately, what I *saw* in her.

11. Shortly after her older brother died, Chloe (who had just celebrated her eighth birthday) went through a deeply philosophical stage. 'I began to question everything,' she told me, 'I had to figure out what death was, that's enough to turn anyone into a philosopher.' One of her great obsessions, to which allusions were still made in her family, concerned thoughts familiar to readers of Descartes and Berkeley. Chloe would put her hand over her eyes and tell the family her brother was still alive because she could see him in her mind just as well as she could see them. Why did they tell her he was dead if she could see him in her own mind? Then, in a further challenge to reality and because of the way she felt towards them, Chloe would (with the grin of a six-year-old child facing the power of its hostile impulses) tell her parents she could kill them by shutting her eyes and never thinking of them again – a plan which no doubt elicited a profoundly unphilosophical response from the parents.

12. Yet solipsism has its limits. Were my views of Chloe anywhere near reality, or had I completely lost judgement? Certainly she *seemed* lovable to me, but was she *actually* as lovable as I thought? It was the old Cartesian colour problem: a bus may *seem* red to a viewer, but is this bus actually red in and of its essence? When Will met Chloe a few weeks later, he certainly had his doubts, unexpressed of course, but

evident from the way he took little interest in her, boring her instead with a lengthy account of how he had once built a cantilevered roof for a villa in La Jolla, and in the way he told me at work the next day that for a Californian, English women were of course 'very special'.

13. To be honest, Chloe gave me the occasional doubt herself. One night, I remember her sitting in my living room reading while we listened to a Bach cantata I had put on. The music sang of heavenly fires, Lord's blessings, and beloved companions, while Chloe's face, tired, but happy, bathed by a streak of light crossing the darkened room from the desk lamp, seemed as though it belonged to an angel, an angel who was only elaborately pretending (with trips to Safeway or the post office) that she was an ordinary mortal, but whose mind was in fact filled with delicate and divine thoughts.

14. Because only the body is open to the eye, the hope of the infatuated lover is that the soul is faithful to its casing, that the body owns an appropriate soul, that what the skin *represents* turns out to be what it *is*. I did not love Chloe *for* her body, I loved her body for the promise of who she was. It was a most inspiring promise.

15. Yet what if her face was only a trompe l'œil? *'By forty, everyone has the face they deserve,'* wrote George Orwell, but Chloe was only just twenty-four – and even if she had been older, we are in truth, despite Orwell's optimistic belief in

natural justice, as unlikely to be given the face we deserve as
the money or the opportunities.

16. 'Can't you turn off this impossible yodelling,' said the
angel all of a sudden.
     'What impossible yodelling?'
     'You know, the music.'
     'It's Bach.'
     'I know, but it sounds so silly, I can't concentrate on
Cosmo.'

17. Is it really *her* I love, I thought to myself as I looked
again at Chloe reading on the sofa across the room, or simply
an idea that collects itself around her mouth, her eyes, her
face? In using her face as a guide to her soul, was I not perhaps guilty of mistaken metonymy, whereby an attribute of
an entity is substituted for the entity itself (the crown for
the monarchy, the wheel for the car, the White House for the
US government, Chloe's angelic expression for Chloe . . .)?

18. In the oasis complex, the thirsty man imagines he
sees water, palm trees, and shade not because he has evidence
for the belief, but because he has a need for it. Desperate
needs bring about a hallucination of their solution: thirst
hallucinates water, the need for love hallucinates a prince or
princess. The oasis complex is never a complete delusion: the
man in the desert does see *something* on the horizon. It is just
that the palms have withered, the well is dry, and the place
is infected with locusts.

19. Was I not victim of a similar delusion, alone in a room with a woman who wore the face of someone composing *The Divine Comedy* while working her way through the *Cosmopolitan* astrology column?

12

Scepticism and Faith

1. By contrast with the history of love, the history of philosophy shows a relentless concern with the discrepancy between appearance and reality. 'I think I see a tree outside,' the philosopher mutters, 'but is it not possible that this is just an optical illusion behind my own retina?' 'I think I see my wife,' mutters the philosopher, adding hopefully, 'but is it not possible that she too is just an optical illusion?'

2. Philosophers tend to limit epistemological doubt to the existence of tables, chairs, the courtyards of Cambridge colleges, and the occasional unwanted wife. But to extend these questions to things that matter to us, to love, for instance, is to raise the frightening possibility that the loved one is but an inner fantasy, with little connection to any objective reality.

3. Doubt is easy when it is not a matter of survival: we are as sceptical as we can afford to be, and it is easiest to be sceptical about things that do not fundamentally sustain us. It is easy to doubt the existence of a table, it is hell to doubt the legitimacy of love.

4. At the start of Western philosophical thinking, the progress from ignorance to knowledge finds itself likened by Plato to a glorious journey from a dark cave into bright sunlight. Men are born unable to perceive reality, Plato tells us, much like cave dwellers who mistake shadows of objects thrown up on the walls for the objects themselves. Only with much effort may illusions be thrown off, and the journey made from the shadowy world into bright sunlight, where things can at last be seen for what they truly are. As with all allegories, this is a tale with a moral: that truth is always superior to illusion.

5. It takes another twenty-three centuries or so until the Socratic assumption about the benefits of pursuing truth is challenged from a practical rather than simply a moral or epistemological standpoint. Everyone from Aristotle to Kant had criticized Plato on the *way* to reach the truth, but no one had seriously questioned the *value* of the undertaking. But in his *Beyond Good and Evil* (1886), Friedrich Nietzsche finally took the bull by the horns and asked:

> What in us really wants 'truth'? . . . We ask the value of this . . . Why not rather untruth? and uncertainty? even ignorance? . . . The falseness of a judgement is not necessarily an objection to it . . . the question is to what extent it is life-advancing; and our fundamental tendency is to assert that the falsest judgements . . . are the most indispensable to us . . . that to renounce false judgements would be to renounce life, would be to deny life.*

---

* *Beyond Good and Evil*, Friedrich Nietzsche (Penguin, 1990).

6. From a religious point of view, the value of truth had of course been placed into question many centuries before. The philosopher Pascal (1623–62, hunchback Jansenist and author of the *Pensées*) had talked of a choice facing every Christian in a world unevenly divided between the horror of a universe without God and the blissful – but infinitely more remote – alternative that God did exist. Even though the odds were in favour of God not existing, Pascal argued that religious faith could still be justified because the joys of the slimmer probability so far outweighed the abomination of the larger one. And so it should perhaps be with love. Lovers cannot remain philosophers for long, they should give way to the religious impulse, which is to believe and have faith, as opposed to the philosophic impulse, which is to doubt and enquire. They should prefer the risk of being *wrong and in love* to being *in doubt and without love*.

7. Such thoughts were running through my mind one evening, sitting on Chloe's bed playing with her toy elephant Guppy. She'd told me that when she was a child, Guppy had played an enormous role in her life. He was a character as real as members of her family, and a lot more sympathetic. He had his own routines, his favourite foods, his own way of sleeping and talking – and yet, from a more dispassionate position, it was evident that Guppy was entirely her creation and had no existence outside her imagination. But if there was one thing that would have been ruinous to Chloe's relationship with the elephant, it would have been to ask her whether or not the creature really existed: *Does this furry thing*

actually live independently of you, or did you not simply invent him? And it occurred to me then that perhaps a similar discretion should be applied to lovers and their beloveds, that one should never ask a lover, *Does this love-stuffed person actually exist or are you simply imagining them?*

8.   Medical history tells us of the case of a man living under the peculiar delusion that he was a fried egg. Quite how or when this idea had entered his head, no one knew, but he now refused to sit down anywhere for fear that he would 'break himself' and 'spill the yolk'. His doctors tried sedatives and other drugs to appease his fears, but nothing seemed to work. Finally, one of them made the effort to enter the mind of the deluded patient and suggested that he should carry a piece of toast with him at all times, which he could place on any chair he wished to sit on, and thereby protect himself from breaking his yolk. From then on, the deluded man was never seen without a piece of toast handy, and was able to continue a more or less normal existence.

9.   What is the point of this story? It merely shows that though one may be living under a delusion (love, the belief that one is an egg), if one finds the complementary part of it (another lover like Chloe under a similar delusion, a piece of toast) then all may be well. Delusions are not harmful in themselves, they only hurt when one is alone in believing in them, when one cannot create an environment in which they can be sustained. So long as both Chloe and I could preserve the yolk of love intact, what did it matter quite what the truth was?

13

Intimacy

1. Watching a cube of sugar dissolve into a cup of camomile tea, Chloe, whose company I relied upon to make my life meaningful, remarked, 'We can't move in together because of my problem: I have to live on my own or else I melt. It's not that I don't want you, it's that I'm afraid of wanting only you, of finding that there's nothing left of me. So excuse it as part of my general screwed-upness, but I'm afraid I have to stay a bag lady.'

2. I had first seen Chloe's bag at Heathrow Airport, a bright pink cylinder with a luminous green shoulder strap. She had arrived at my door with it the first night she came to stay, once more apologizing for its offensive colours, saying she had used it to pack a toothbrush and a set of fresh clothes for the next day. I had assumed the bag would be temporary, but she never gave it up, repacking it every morning as though this might be the last time we would ever see one another, as though to leave even a pair of earrings behind created an unsustainable risk of dissolution.

3. Yet whatever her enthusiasm for independence, with

time Chloe nevertheless began leaving things behind. Not toothbrushes or pairs of shoes, but pieces of herself. It began with language, with Chloe leaving me her way of saying *not ever* instead of never, and of stressing the *be* of *before*, or of saying *take care* before hanging up the telephone. She in turn acquired use of my *perfect* and *if you really think so*. Habits began to leak between us: I acquired Chloe's need for total darkness in the bedroom, she followed my way of folding the newspaper, I took to wandering in circles around the sofa to think a problem through, she acquired a taste for lying on the carpet.

4. Diffusion brought with it intimacy. The borders between us ceased to be strictly patrolled. Our bodies no longer felt watched or judged. Chloe could read in bed and slide a finger into her nostril to clear an obstruction, roll it into a ball till it was dry and hard, and swallow it whole – without needing to hide or apologize. We could risk intervals of silence, we were no longer paranoid talkers, unwilling to let the conversation drop lest tranquillity seem unfaithful. We grew assured of ourselves in the other's mind, rendering perpetual seduction (stemming from a fear of the opposite) obsolete.

5. I got to know not only Chloe's opinions and habits, but also the finer grain of her being: the sound of her voice when she spoke on the phone in the next room, the rumble of her stomach when she was hungry, her expression before a sneeze, the shape of her eyes when she awoke, the way she shook a wet umbrella, and the sound of a brush through her hair.

6. An awareness of each other's particularities gave us a need to rename one another. Chloe and I had met with names given to us by our parents and formalized by passports and birth registers and naturally found that the more private knowledge we had acquired of one another deserved to find expression (however oblique) in names that others didn't use. Whereas in her office, Chloe was Chloe, to me, for reasons neither of us ever quite understood, she became known simply as *Tidge*. For my part, because I had once amused her with talk of a word for the pessimistic outlook of German intellectuals, I became known, perhaps less mysteriously, as *Weltschmerz*. The importance of these nicknames lay not in the particular name we had landed on – we might have ended up calling one another *Pwitt* and *Tic* – but in the fact that we had chosen to relabel one another. *Tidge* suggested a knowledge of Chloe that Roy in accounts did not possess (the knowledge of the sound of a brush through her hair). Whereas *Chloe* belonged to her civil status, *Tidge* lay beyond the ordinary social realm, in the more secret and unique folds of love.

7. In each other's company, we spent a good deal of time discussing how awful other people were. Unable to express ourselves honestly in most of our daily interactions, we could between us aerate our lies and atone for the social niceties we had performed. Chloe became the final repository of my harsh verdicts on friends or colleagues. Things I had long thought about them but had tried to deny, I was free to share with a sympathetic and even encouraging audience.

We frequently indulged in orgies of gossip. Whatever the pleasures of discovering mutual loves, nothing compares with the intimacy of landing on mutual hates. At times, we came close to concluding (though coyness prevented us from quite admitting this openly) that everyone we'd ever come across was deeply flawed – and that we were in truth the only decent humans left on the planet. Love nourished itself through perpetual criticism of outsiders. The finest proof of our loyalty towards one other was our monstrous disloyalties towards everyone else.

8.   We retreated into each other's company to laugh at the hypocrisy demanded by society. We returned from formal work dinners and mocked the accents and opinions of those to whom we had politely said goodbye minutes before. We might in bed replay a conversation we had just had. I would impersonate a bearded journalist Chloe had spoken to, she would reply as she had done originally, all this while she masturbated me beneath the sheets. I would pretend to be shocked to find Chloe's hand where it was and ask her in the tone of a virginal parson: '*Madam, what on earth are you doing with my honourable member?*' '*Sir,*' she would reply like an aristocratic lady in a period drama, '*I have no idea how this dishonourable member ever came to be in my sight.*' Or she would leap out of bed and scream, '*Sir, please leave my bed immediately, or I will have to call my manservant Bernard.*' In our intimacy, social formalities found themselves rerun in a comic light, like a tragedy which is spoofed by the actors backstage, the actor playing Hamlet seizing Gertrude after the perfor-

mance and shouting through the dressing room, 'Fuck me, Mummy!'

9.   We even started to acquire a story. Love seems indispensably connected to stories. 'One day, a boy met a girl' is enough for an audience to start to want to know what happened next. Powering most love stories are obstacles. Paul and Virginie, Anna and Vronsky, Tarzan and Jane tend to struggle against odds that confirm and enrich their bond. In a jungle, on a shipwrecked boat or the side of a mountain, the classic romantic couple proves the strength of its love by the vigour with which it overcomes adversities.

10.   But there wasn't much adventure or struggle around to be had. The world that Chloe and I lived in had largely been stripped of capacities for epic conflict. Our parents didn't care, the jungle had been tamed, society hid its disapproval behind universal tolerance, restaurants stayed open late, credit cards were accepted almost everywhere, and sex was a duty, not a crime. Yet Chloe and I did have a modest story of our own, a set of common experiences that bonded us together. What is an experience? Something that breaks a polite routine and for a brief period allows us to witness things with the heightened sensitivity afforded to us by novelty, danger, or beauty – and it's on the basis of shared experiences that intimacy is given an opportunity to grow. Friendships nourished solely by occasional dinners will never have the depth of those forged on a trek or at a university. Two people who are surprised by a lion in a jungle clearing

will – unless one of them is eaten – be effectively bonded by what they have seen.

11. Chloe and I were never surprised by a predator, but we lived through a host of small urban experiences. Returning from a party one warm summer's night, we came across a dead body. The corpse lay on the corner of Charlwood Street and Belgrave Road. It was a beautiful young woman who looked at first as though she had collapsed drunk on the pavement. But as we were about to pass her, Chloe noticed the handle of a knife sticking out of her stomach. How much does one know of someone till one has seen a corpse with them? We kneeled down over the body, Chloe took on the voice of a pilot commandeering an agitated or plain hysterical crew (me) during an emergency landing, told me not to look, got me to call the police, checked the woman's pulse, and carefully left everything as she had found it. I felt in awe of her professionalism, though in the middle of police questioning she broke into uncontrollable sobbing and was unable to banish the image of the knife handle for several weeks. It was a barbaric incident, but one that served to unite us. We spent the rest of the night awake, drinking whisky in my apartment, telling each other a series of increasingly macabre and silly stories, impersonating policemen and corpses with kitchen knives in order to exorcize our fears.

12. A few months later, we were in a bagel shop in Brick Lane, when an elegant man in a pinstripe suit next to us in the queue silently handed Chloe a crumpled note, on which

was scrawled in large letters the words: '*I love you.*' Chloe opened the piece of paper, swallowed hard on reading it, then looked back at the man who had given it to her. But he had chosen to act as though nothing had happened and simply stared out at the street with the dignified expression of a man in a pinstripe suit. So just as innocently, Chloe folded the note and slipped it into her pocket. The bizarreness of the incident meant that, as with the corpse only more light-heartedly, it became something of a leitmotif in our relationship, an incident in our story to which we constantly alluded. In restaurants, we would occasionally silently slip one another notes with all the mystery of the man in the bagel shop, but with only the message *Please pass the salt* written on them. For anyone watching, it must have seemed odd and incomprehensible to see us collapsing into giggles. But the essence of leitmotifs is that they refer back to incidents others cannot understand because they were absent from the founding scene. No wonder if such self-referential, egotistical behaviour drives those standing on the sidelines to distraction.

13. There were plenty of other joint experiences – people we had encountered or things we had seen, done, or heard – which helped to create a common heritage. There was a psychoanalyst we met at a dinner who told Chloe that he was currently sleeping with two of his patients. There was my friend Will Knott who, having initially taken little interest in Chloe, started sending her obscure books on architecture accompanied by quizzical notes ('Who can say how long each

of us will stand??!' ran one, appended to *Steel – the Material of the Future*). There was the toy giraffe we bought in Bath to keep Chloe's elephant company on the bed and ended up calling Geoffrey after a long-necked colleague of Chloe's at work. And there was a meeting with an accountant on a train who confessed she always carried a gun in her handbag.

14. Interest did not naturally belong to such anecdotes. For the most part, only Chloe and I appreciated them, because of the subsidiary associations we attached to them. Yet these leitmotifs were important because they gave us the feeling that we were far from strangers to one another, that we had lived through things together, and remembered the joint meanings we had derived from them. However slight these leitmotifs were, they acted like cement. The language of intimacy they helped to create was a reminder that (without clearing our way through jungles, slaying dragons, or even sharing apartments) Chloe and I had created something of a world together.

14

'I'-Confirmation

1. Late one Sunday in the middle of July, we were sitting in a cafe at the unkempt end of the Portobello Road. It had been a beautiful day, spent largely in Hyde Park, tanning and reading books. But since around five o'clock, I had been sliding into depression. I felt like going home to hide under the bedclothes. Sunday evenings had long saddened me, reminders of death, unfinished business, guilt, and loss. We had been sitting in silence, Chloe reading the papers, I gazing through the window at the traffic and people outside. Suddenly she leaned over, gave me a kiss, and whispered, 'You're wearing your lost orphan boy look again.' No one had ever ascribed such an expression to me before, though when Chloe mentioned it, it at once accorded with and alleviated the confused sadness I happened to be feeling at the time. I felt an intense (and perhaps disproportionate) love for her on account of that remark, because of her awareness of what I had been feeling but had been unable to formulate myself, for her willingness to enter my world and objectify it for me – a gratefulness for reminding the orphan that he is an orphan, and hence returning him home.

2. Perhaps it is true that we do not really exist until there is someone there to see us existing, we cannot properly speak until there is someone there who can understand what we are saying, in essence, we are not wholly alive until we are loved.

3. What does it mean that man is a 'social animal'? Only that humans need one another in order to define themselves and achieve self-consciousness, in a way that molluscs or earthworms do not. We cannot come to a proper sense of ourselves if there aren't others around to show us what we're like. 'A man can acquire anything in solitude except a character,' wrote Stendhal, suggesting that character has its genesis in the reactions of others to our words and actions. Our selves are fluid and require the contours provided by our neighbours. To feel whole, we need people in the vicinity who know us as well, sometimes better, than we know ourselves.

4. Without love, we lose the ability to possess a proper identity, within love, there is a constant confirmation of our selves. It is no wonder that the concept of a God who can see us has been central to many religions: to be seen is to be assured that we exist, all the better if one is dealing with a God (or partner) who *loves* us. Surrounded by people who precisely do *not* remember who we are, people to whom we often relate our stories and yet who will repeatedly forget how many times we have been married, how many children we have, and whether our name is Brad or Bill, Catrina or Catherine (and we forget much the same about them), is it not comforting to be able to find refuge from the dangers of

invisibility in the arms of someone who has our identity firmly in mind?

5.   It is no coincidence if, semantically speaking, love and interest are almost interchangeable, 'I love butterflies' meaning much the same as 'I am interested in butterflies'. To love someone is to take a deep interest in them, and by such concern to bring them to a richer sense of what they are doing and saying. Through her understanding, Chloe's behaviour towards me gradually became studded with elements of what could be termed 'I'-*confirmation*. Contained in her understanding of many of my moods, in her knowledge of my tastes, in the things she told me about myself, in her memory of my routines and habits, and in her humorous acknowledgement of my phobias lay a multitude of varied 'I'-*confirmations*. Chloe noticed that I was a hypochondriac, that I was shy and hated speaking on the phone, was obsessive in my need to get eight hours' sleep a night, hated lingering in restaurants at the end of meals, used politeness as an aggressive defence, and preferred to say 'maybe' rather than yes or no. She would quote me back at myself ('*Last time, you said you didn't like that kind of irony . . .*'), patiently holding in mind elements – both good and bad – of my character ('*You always panic whenever . . .*' '*I've never seen anyone forget petrol as often as you do . . .*'). I was afforded a chance to mature thanks to the insights into my personality that Chloe afforded me. It takes the intimacy of a lover to point out facets of character that others simply don't bother with. There were times when Chloe would tell me frankly that I was defensive

or critical, or more colourfully, 'a jumped-up twerp' or 'as nasty as congealed gravy' – and I would be brought face to face with areas of myself that ordinary introspection (in the interests of inner harmony) would have avoided, that others would have been too uninterested to highlight, and that it needed the honesty of the bedroom to reveal.

6.   Happiness with other people seems bounded by two kinds of excess: suffocation and loneliness. Chloe had always felt the former to be the greater danger. Oppressed by the judgemental and controlling attitudes of her parents, at school she had dreamt of spending time wholly on her own – and in her year off before university, flew to Arizona on the proceeds of money she had saved up from years of holiday and Saturday jobs. She rented a cabin on the edge of a tiny town she had picked almost at random on a map. She acquired a shelf full of books that she'd always longed to read, and which she intended to work her way through as she watched the sun rise and set over the moonscape. But within a few weeks of arriving, she began to feel the solitude that she had longed for all her life start to work a disorienting and frightening effect on her. The sound of her own voice came as a shock when she heard it in the shops. Her books felt remote and unengaging. She took to staring at herself in the mirror to retain a sense of being. She felt paranoid and ethereal. After only a month, she abruptly decided to leave her cabin for a job as a waitress in a restaurant in Phoenix, unable to bear any longer the feeling of unreality that had descended on her. When she reached Phoenix, social contact was like

water to a parched survivor. She launched into conversations whenever she could, delighting in the comfort offered by the simplest exchanges.

7. It was a long time before I was in any position to help Chloe to feel understood. Only slowly did I begin to unearth, from among the millions of words she spoke and actions she performed, the great themes of her life. In our knowledge of others, we are necessarily forced to interpret clues, we are like detectives or archaeologists who piece together stories from fragments, tracing the origins of a murder from a kitchen towel and a lemon squeezer or a civilization from a gardening implement and an earring. I often got it wrong. For example, it was a while before I quite appreciated the role of self-denial in her life. One morning in my flat, as we were having breakfast, she told me she had been ill in the night, had crept out of bed and driven to a chemist, all without waking me up. My first reaction was bewildered anger. Why had she not said something? Was our relationship really so distant that she couldn't wake me up even in a crisis? But my anger (only a form of jealousy) was crude, it failed to take into account what I only gradually learnt: how deep-seated and pervasive was Chloe's inclination to suffer in silence. She would have to have been near death before waking me, for everything about her wished not to place responsibility on others. Once I had located this strand in her nature, other aspects could be understood as related manifestations of it: her lack of acknowledged anger towards her parents (an anger that allowed itself expression only in savage irony), her

self-deprecation, her harshness towards self-pitying people, her sense of duty, even her way of crying (muted sobs rather than hysterical wailing).

8. Like a telephone engineer sitting on the edge of a manhole with a jumble of cables in his lap, I slowly learnt to identify some key threads in Chloe's personality. I began to recognize her hatred of stinginess every time we were in a group in a restaurant. I began sensing her desire not to be trapped, the desert-escapist side of her nature. I admired her constant visual creativity, which showed itself not just in her work, but in the way she would lay the table or arrange a bowl of flowers. I began detecting her awkwardness with other women and her greater ease with men. I recognized her fierce loyalty to those she considered her friends, an instinctive sense of clan and community. With such characteristics, Chloe slowly assumed a complex coherence in my mind, someone with consistency and a degree of predictability, someone whose tastes in a film or a person I could now begin to guess without asking.

9. The problem with needing others to legitimate our existence is that we are very much at their mercy to have a *correct* identity ascribed to us. If, as Stendhal says, we lack a character without others, then the other with whom we share our bed must be a skilled intermediary or we will end up feeling deformed and misrepresented. But do not others by definition always distort us – whether for better or worse?

10.   Everyone returns us to a different sense of ourselves, for we become a little of who they think we are. Our selves could be compared to an amoeba, whose outer walls are elastic, and therefore adapt to the environment. It is not that the amoeba has no *dimensions*, simply that it has no self-defined *shape*. It is my absurdist side that an absurdist person will draw out of me, and my seriousness that a serious person will evoke. If someone thinks I am shy, I will probably end up shy, if someone thinks me funny, I am likely to keep cracking jokes.

11.   When Chloe had lunch with my parents, she was silent throughout the meal. I later asked her what was wrong, but she herself couldn't understand. She had tried to be lively and yet the suspicions of the two strangers facing her across the table had stopped her from expanding into her usual self. My parents had not been overtly nasty, yet their stiffness had prevented Chloe from rising above monosyllabicity. It was a reminder that the labelling of others is usually a silent process. Most people do not openly force us into roles, they merely suggest that we adopt them through their reactions to us, and hence surreptitiously prevent us from moving beyond whatever mould they have assigned us.

12.   A few years before, Chloe had for a time gone out with an academic at London University. The analytical philosopher, who had written five books and contributed to many scholarly journals, had left her with a sense of total mental inadequacy. How had he done this? Chloe couldn't tell. Without ever expressly saying anything critical, he had succeeded

in shaping the amoeba according to his preconceptions, namely, that Chloe was a beautiful young student who should leave matters of the mind to him. And so, like a self-fulfilling prophecy, Chloe had begun unconsciously acting on the verdict of her character, handed out like a covert end-of-term report by the wise philosopher who had written five books and contributed to many scholarly journals. She had ended up feeling exactly as stupid as she was believed to be.

13. Children are always described from a third-person perspective (*'Isn't Chloe a cute/ugly/intelligent/stupid kid?'*) before they gain the ability to influence their own definitions. Overcoming childhood could be understood as an attempt to correct the false stories of others. But the struggle against distortion continues beyond childhood. Most people get us wrong, either out of neglect or prejudice. Even being loved implies a gross bias – a pleasant distortion, but a distortion nevertheless. Like Narcissus, we are doomed to disappointment in gazing at our reflection in the watery eyes of another. *No eye can wholly contain our 'I'*. We will always be chopped off in some area or other, fatally or not.

14. When I told Chloe my idea that people's personalities in relationships were a bit like amoebas, she laughed and told me she'd loved drawing amoebas at school.

'Here, give me the newspaper,' she said, reaching in her bag for a pencil. 'I'll draw you the difference between what shape my amoeba-self has at the office and what shape it has with you.'

Then she drew the following:

Office Chloeba

Home Chloeba

'What are all the wiggly bits?' I asked.

'Oh, that's because I feel wiggly around you.'

'What?'

'Well, you know, you give me space. I feel more complicated than in the office. You're interested in me and you understand me better, so that's why I made it wiggly, so that it's sort of natural.'

'OK, I see, so what's this straight side?'

'Where?'

'Up in the north-west of the amoeba.'

'You know I never did much geography. But yeah, I think I see it. Well, you don't understand *everything* about me, do you? So I thought I'd better make it more realistic. The straight line is all the sides of me you don't understand or don't have time for and stuff.'

'Oh.'

'Christ, don't make that long face, you wouldn't want to know what could happen if that line went squiggly! And don't worry, if it was that serious, I wouldn't be squidged here with you being such a happy amoeba.'

15. What did Chloe mean by her amoebic straight line? Just that I could not wholly understand her, an unsurprising but still sobering reminder of the limits of empathy. What was frustrating my efforts? Perhaps that I was constrained to fathoming her through my existing conceptions of human nature. My knowledge of her was necessarily filtered through my own past. Like a European who orients himself in a Rocky Mountain landscape by saying, 'This looks just like Switzerland,' I might only have grasped the source of one of Chloe's depressed moods by thinking, '*It's because she's feeling x . . . like my sister when . . .*' To comprehend her, I had to rely on an understanding of human nature that had been shaped by my biology, class, and psychological biography.

16. To illustrate how we can only ever pick up on certain elements in our beloveds' characters, we might compare the way we look at them to a barbecue skewer. For instance, I was able to skewer (or appreciate or relate) to Chloe's:

> — *irony* — *colour of eyes* — *gap between two front teeth* — *intellect* — *talent for baking bread* — *relationship with her mother* — *social anxiety* — *love of Beethoven* — *hatred of laziness* — *taste for camomile tea* — *objection to snobbery* — *love of woollen clothes* — *claustrophobia* — *desire for honesty* →

Yet this was far from comprising everything about her. Had
I been a different barbecue skewer, I might have had more
time for her:

> — *interest in healthy eating* — *ankles* — *love of outdoor
> markets* — *mathematical talent* — *relationship with her brother*
> — *love of nightclubs* — *thoughts on God* — *enthusiasm for rice*
> — *Degas* — *skating* — *long country walks* — *objection to
> music in the car* — *taste for Victorian architecture* →

17. Though I felt myself attentive to the complexities of
Chloe's nature, I must have been guilty of great abbreviations, of passing lightly over areas I simply did not have the
empathy or maturity to understand. I was responsible for
the greatest but most unavoidable abbreviation of all, that of
only being able to participate in Chloe's life as an outsider,
someone whose inner world I could imagine, but never
directly experience. However close we might be, Chloe was
in the end *another human being*, with all the mystery and
distance this implied, the inevitable distance embodied in
the thought that we must die alone.

18. We long for a love in which we are never reduced or
misunderstood. We have a morbid resistance to classifica-
tion by others, to others placing labels on us (the man, the
woman, the rich one, the poor one, the Jew, the Catholic,
etc.). To ourselves, we are after all always *un-labelable*. When
alone, we are always simply 'me', and shift between sides of
ourselves effortlessly and without the constraints imposed
by the preconceptions of others. But hearing Chloe one day

talk of '*this guy I was seeing a while back*', I was saddened to imagine myself in a few years' time (another man facing her across the tuna salad) being described merely as '*this architect guy I was once seeing* . . .' Her casual reference to a past lover provided the necessary objectification for me to realize that, however special I was to her, I still existed within certain definitions ('a guy', 'my boyfriend') – and that in Chloe's eyes, I was necessarily a simplified version of myself.

19. But as we must be labelled, characterized, and defined by others, the person we end up loving is the *good-enough barbecue skewerer*, the person who loves us for more or less the things we deem ourselves to be lovable for, who understands us for more or less the things we need to be understood for. That Chloeba and I were together implied that, for the moment at least, we had been given enough room to expand in the ways our complexities demanded.

15

Intermittences of the Heart

1. The stories we tell are always too simple. I was a man in love with a woman, but how much of the mobility and inconstancy of my emotions could such a sentence hope to carry? Was there room in it for all the infidelity, boredom, irritation, and indifference that was often knitted together with this love? Could any simple account accurately reflect the degree of ambivalence to which all relationships seem fated? Chloe and I lived a love story stretching over an expanse of time during which our feelings gyrated so much that to talk of being simply *in love* was, though reassuring, a desperately crude foreshortening of events.

2. One weekend, we went to Bath. At work the day after, when someone asked what I'd been up to, I replied, *'We had a great couple of days in Bath.'* Even in my own mind, the story of what had occurred grew elementary and facile. I remembered a beautiful sandy-coloured town and a blue sky. I remembered being happy, I remembered Chloe saying that I was a better, different sort of person on holiday. And yet if I now force myself to think back, to tell more than a one-line story, then I start to recall a more complicated set of events

pullulating beneath the surface of the trip, events which it might take four hundred pages to describe properly. To make a stab, I remember that shortly after our arrival, Chloe and I had an argument about what room we'd take in the hotel. I suggested we make a fuss about the one we were initially offered because I didn't like the curtains and there was a strange dripping sound in the bathroom. Chloe called me 'no longer endearingly insane'. On a walk around the abbey, I became preoccupied with my professional life and wished that I'd chosen a different career that paid more. When Chloe asked me what was wrong, I told her I was jealous of Will for all the attention he was getting among our peers. In the evening, Chloe declined to have sex, saying it was her period, though I suspected this had ended a bit earlier. The next day, in a restaurant called John Wood the Elder, I was drawn to a beautiful girl with glasses sitting near us and irrationally engineered an argument with Chloe about wildlife reserves to punish her for her inadvertent role in preventing me from kissing the stranger (who didn't seem sad about what she was missing out on), while on the way to the station, Chloe mysteriously flirted with a cross-eyed taxi driver, telling him that she loved showing off her belly-button in summer, which resulted in a sulk on my part that didn't end till we reached Paddington Station three hours later.

3. Perhaps we can forgive ourselves for telling simple stories which sum up weekends with the word *pleasant*, stories which thereby introduce order into events which are in fact made up of tissues of troubling and ambivalent feelings. Yet

perhaps we also owe it to ourselves occasionally to face the flux beneath the abbreviations. I *loved* Chloe – and yet how much more variegated the reality was.

4. When her friend Alice invited us to dinner one Friday night, Chloe accepted and predicted that I would fall in love with her. There were eight of us around Alice's dining table, everyone jogging elbows as they tried to bring the food to their mouths over a table built for four. Alice lived alone in the top floor of a house in Balham, worked as a secretary at the Arts Council, and I had to admit, I did fall a little in love with her.

5. However happy we may be with our partner, our love for them necessarily hinders us from pursuing alternatives. Why should this constrain us if we love them? Why should we feel this as a loss unless our love for them has already begun to wane? Because in resolving our need to *love*, we do not always succeed in resolving our need to *long*.

6. Watching Alice talk, light a candle that had blown out, rush into the kitchen with the plates and brush a strand of blonde hair from her face, I found myself falling victim to romantic nostalgia, which descends whenever we are faced with those who might have been our lovers, but whom chance has decreed we will never properly know. The possibility of an alternative love story is a reminder that the life we are leading is only one of a myriad of possible lives and it is the impossibility of leading them all that plunges

us into sadness. There is a longing for a return to a time without the need for choices, free of the regret at the inevitable loss that all choice (however wonderful) has entailed.

7. In city streets, I would often be made aware of hundreds (and by implication even millions) of women whose lives were running concurrently with mine, but who were fated to remain a mystery to me. Though I loved Chloe, the sight of these women occasionally filled me with such regret, it seemed like the only solution might be to tell them how I felt and thus alleviate the burden of sadness (I resisted the impulse). Standing on a train platform or in the line at the bank I would catch sight of a given face, perhaps overhear a snatch of conversation (the woman's car had broken down, she was graduating from university, her mother was ill . . .), and feel torn apart by being unable to know the rest of the story and kiss its protagonist.

8. I could have chatted to Alice on the sofa after dinner, but something made me reluctant to do anything but dream. Alice's face evoked a void inside of me with no clear dimensions or intentions and that my love for Chloe had somehow not resolved. The unknown carries with it a mirror of all our deepest, most inexpressible wishes. The unknown is the fatal proposition that a face seen across the room will always hold out to the known. I may have loved Chloe but because I *knew* Chloe, I did not *long* for her. Longing cannot indefinitely direct itself at those we know, for their qualities are charted and therefore lack the mystery longing demands. A face seen

for a few moments or hours only then to disappear for ever is the necessary catalyst for dreams that cannot be formulated, a desire that seems as indefinable as it is unquenchable.

9. 'So, did you fall in love with her?' Chloe asked in the car.
'Of course not.'
'She's your type.'
'No, she isn't. And anyway, you know I'm in love with you.'

In the typical scenario of betrayal, one partner asks the other, 'How could you have betrayed me with *x* when you said you loved *me*?' But there is no inconsistency between a betrayal and a declaration of love if time is taken into the equation. 'I love you' can only ever be taken to mean *'for now'*. I was not lying to Chloe, but my words were time-bound promises, a truth too disturbing for most relationships fully to take on board, or else couples would have little to talk about other than their fluctuating feelings.

10. I was not only imaginatively unfaithful, I was also often bored. As inhabitants of luxury hotels and palaces attest, one can get used to anything. For periods, I entirely ceased to notice the miracle that was Chloe's love for me. She became a normal and hence invisible feature of my life.

11. Then would come moments when I'd recover the ability to see her as I had done in the early days of our love story. One weekend, on a visit to Winchester, we broke down on the motorway and called the AA for help. When a

van arrived a quarter of an hour later, Chloe went to deal with the mechanic (a primitive impulse had left me unable to talk to him, from a feeling of embarrassment that, though I was a man, I hadn't been able to repair the car, let alone work out how the bonnet opened). Watching her talk to this stranger (he was in leather from tip to toe, for reasons I hoped were strictly related to his professional role), by a form of identification with him, the woman I knew abruptly appeared foreign to me. I looked at her face and heard her voice without the dulling blanket of familiarity, I saw her as she might strike a leather-clad mechanic, I saw her stripped of the normalizing influence of time.

12.   As a result, I was overcome by an urge to tear off her grey-green cardigan and make passionate love to her on the motorway embankment. The disruption of habit had made Chloe unknown and exotic again, desirable like a woman I had never touched, even though she had only that morning walked around my flat naked without arousing any wish in me beyond that of finishing an article I had begun reading on macro-economics in the developing world.

13.   It took the AA man a few minutes to locate the fault, something to do with the battery ('You want to watch your levels, darling,' he had called out to Chloe from behind the bonnet), and we were ready to continue to Winchester. But my desire signalled otherwise.

   'Imagine that you've broken down by the side of the road and I'm this leather-clad stranger who wants to take off your clothes and take you roughly on the embankment, lifting up your innocent flowery skirt and handling you without mercy.'

'Are you sure?'

'With all my loins.'

'Christ, OK. Well, give me a moment to perfect my stranded-without-a-battery-but-extremely-horny expression.'

14. We made love twice on the back seat of Chloe's Volkswagen, in between pieces of luggage and old papers. Though welcome, our sudden and unpredictable ecstasy, the grasping at one another's clothes and the imaginative scenarios (I adopted a Scottish accent for the roadside tryst, she played at being married-but-looking), were reminders of how confusing the flux of passions could be. Capable of being seized off the motorway by desire, might we not drift apart on the back of less compatible thoughts and hormones at a later date?

15. Chloe and I had a joke between us which acknowledged the intermittences of the heart, and eased the demand that love's light burn with the constancy of an electric bulb.

'Is something wrong? Do you not like me today?' one of us would ask.

'I like you less.'

'Really, much less?'

'No, not that much.'

'Out of ten?'

'Today? Oh, probably six and a half or, no, perhaps more six and three-quarters. And how about with you with me?'

'God, I'd say around minus three, though it might have been around twelve and a half earlier this morning when you . . .'

16. In another Chinese restaurant (Chloe loved them), I realized that life with other people functioned a little like the wheel at the centre of the table on which dishes had been placed, and which could be revolved so that one would be faced by shrimp one minute, pork the next. Did loving someone not follow a similar circular pattern, in which there were regular revolutions in the intensity and nature of one's feelings? We tend to remain attached to a fixed view of emotions, as though a line existed between loving and not loving that could only be crossed twice, at the beginning and end of a relationship, rather than commuted across from minute to minute. But in reality, in only a day, I might go around every available emotional dish on my inner Chinese platter. I might feel that Chloe was:

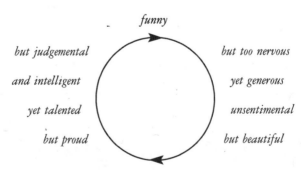

17. I was not alone in my erratic moods, for there were times when Chloe too would unexpectedly display bursts of aggression or frustration. Discussing a film with friends one night, she swerved into a hostile speech about my 'consistently patronizing' attitudes towards other people. I was at first baffled, for I had not even said anything, but I soon guessed that I was being repaid for a previous offence – or even that I had become a useful target for a disgruntlement that Chloe was feeling towards someone else. Many of our arguments had an unfairness to them: I might get furious with Chloe not for the surface reason that she was emptying the dishwasher very noisily when I was trying to watch the news, but because I was feeling guilty about not having answered a difficult business call earlier in the day. Chloe might in turn deliberately make lots of noise in an effort to symbolize an anger she had not communicated to me that morning. We might define maturity as the ability to give everyone what they deserve when they deserve it, to separate the emotions that belong and should be restricted to oneself from those that should at once be expressed to their initiators rather than passed on to later and more innocent arrivals. We were often not mature.

18. If philosophers have traditionally advocated a life lived according to reason, condemning in its name a life led by desire, it is because reason is a bedrock of continuity. Unlike romantics, philosophers do not let their interests veer insanely from Chloe to Alice and back to Chloe again, because stable reasons support the choices they have made.

In love, they will stay constant, their feelings as assured as the trajectory of an arrow in flight.

19. As a result of such reasoning, philosophers can be assured a stable identity, for *who I am* is to a large extent constituted by *what I want*. If the emotional man one day loves Samantha and the next Sally, then who is he? If I went to bed one night loving Chloe, and awoke the next morning indifferent to her, then who was I? Yet I was also faced with the intractable problem of locating solid *reasons* for either loving or not-loving Chloe. Objectively, there were no compelling reasons to do either, which made my occasional ambivalence towards her all the more irresolvable. Had there been sound, unassailable reasons to love or hate, there would have been benchmarks to return to. But just as the gap between two front teeth had never been a reason to fall head over heels in love with someone, so opinions on wildlife reserves was never a fair basis for hating them.

20. Tempering our ambivalence was a contrary pull towards stability and continuity, which reined us in whenever there was an urge to develop romantic subplots or digress from our love story. Waking up from an erotic dream I had spent in the company of a woman who was a blend of two faces I had seen at a conference on solar energy the day before, I at once relocated myself emotionally on finding Chloe beside me. I stereotyped my possibilities, I returned to the role assigned to me by my status as a boyfriend, I bowed to the tremendous authority of what already exists.

21. Tempests within the couple were also kept in check by the more stable assumptions that others around us held about our relationship. I remember a furious row that erupted a few minutes before we were due to meet friends for coffee one Saturday. At the time, we both felt this row to be so serious, we imagined breaking up over it. Yet this possibility was curtailed by the arrival of friends who could not remotely envisage such a thing. Over coffee, there were questions directed at the couple, which betrayed no knowledge of the possibility of rupture and hence helped to avoid it. The presence of others moderated our mood swings. When we were unsure of where we were going, we could hide beneath the comforting analysis of those who stood on the outside, aware only of the continuities, unaware that there was nothing inviolable about our plot line.

22. We also found comfort in planning the future. Because there was a threat that love might end as suddenly as it had begun, we tried to reinforce the present through an appeal to a common destiny. We dreamt of where we would live and how many children we would have, we identified ourselves with the wrinkled couples taking their grandchildren for walks and holding hands in Kensington Gardens. Defending ourselves against love's demise, we took pleasure in planning a mutual future in precise detail. There were houses we both liked near Kentish Town and together decorated in our heads, completing them with two small studies at the top, a large fitted kitchen with the sleekest appliances in the basement, and a garden full of flowers and trees. Though we

had not discussed marriage in any concrete way, we had to believe that there was no reason why we might not contractually bind our hearts together. How is it possible to love someone and at the same time imagine decorating a house with someone else? It was indispensable that we contemplate what it would be like to grow old together and retire with our dentures to a bungalow by the sea.

23. My dislike of talking about ex-lovers with Chloe stemmed from a related fear of inconstancy. Ex-lovers were reminders that situations I had at one point thought to be permanent had proved not to be so. From within a relationship, there is infinite cruelty in the idea of one's indifference towards past loves. One evening, in the bookshop of the Hayward Gallery, I caught sight of an old girlfriend, leafing through a biography of Giacometti across the room. Chloe was a few steps away from me, searching for some postcards to send to friends. Giacometti had meant much to this ex-girlfriend and me. I could easily have gone to say hello. After all, I had met several of Chloe's former lovers, one or two of whom she saw on a regular basis. But my discomfort was too deep: the woman evoked a fickleness in myself, and by extension and just as importantly in Chloe, that I lacked the courage to face.

24. There is something appalling in the idea that a person for whom you would sacrifice anything today might in a few months cause you to cross a road or a bookshop. If my love for Chloe constituted the essence of my self at that moment,

then the definitive end of my love for her would mean nothing less than the death of a part of me.

25. If Chloe and I continued despite all this to believe we were in love, it was perhaps because the affection far outweighed the boredom and indifference. Yet we always remained aware that what we had chosen to call love might be an abbreviation for a far more complex, and ultimately less palatable, reality.

16

The Fear of Happiness

1. One of love's greatest drawbacks is that, for a while at least, it is in danger of making us seriously happy.

2. Chloe and I chose to travel to Spain in the final week of August – travel (like love) an attempt to follow a dream into reality. In London, we had read the brochures of Utopia Travel, specialists in the Spanish rental market, and had settled for a converted farmhouse in the village of Aras de Alpuente, in the mountains behind Valencia. The house looked better in reality than it had in the photographs. The rooms were simply but comfortably furnished, the bathroom worked, there was a terrace shaded by vine leaves, a lake nearby to swim in, and a farmer next door who kept a goat and welcomed us with a gift of olive oil and cheese.

3. We had arrived in the late afternoon, having hired a car at the airport and driven up the narrow mountain roads. We immediately went for a swim, diving into the clear blue waters and drying off in the dying sun. Then we had returned to the house and sat on the terrace with a bottle of wine and olives to watch the sun set behind the hills.

'Isn't it wonderful,' I remarked lyrically.

'Isn't it?' echoed Chloe.

'But is it?' I joked.

'Shush, you're ruining the scene.'

'No, I'm serious, it really is wonderful. I could never have imagined a place like this existing. It seems so cut off from everything, like a paradise no one's bothered to ruin.'

'I could spend the rest of my life here,' sighed Chloe.

'So could I.'

'We could live here together, I'd tend the goats, you'd handle the olives, we'd write books, paint, and fa . . .'

'Are you all right?' I asked, seeing Chloe suddenly wince with pain.

'Yeah, I am now. I don't know what happened. I just got this terrible pain in my head, like an awful throbbing or something. It's probably nothing. Ah, no, shit, there it comes again.'

'Let me feel.'

'You won't be able to feel anything, it's inside.'

'I know, but I'll empathize.'

'God, I'd better lie down. It's probably just the travelling, or the height, or something. But I'd better go inside. You stay out here, I'll be fine.'

4. Chloe's pains did not get better. She took an aspirin and went to bed, but she was unable to sleep. Unsure of how seriously to take her suffering, but worried that her natural tendency to play everything down meant it was probably extremely serious, I decided to get a doctor. The farmer and

his wife were in their cottage eating dinner when I knocked and asked in fragments of Spanish where the nearest doctor could be found. It turned out he lived in Villar del Arzobispo, a village some twenty kilometres away.

5. Dr Saavedra was immensely dignified for a country doctor. He wore a white linen suit, had spent a term at Imperial College in the 1950s, was a lover of the English theatrical tradition, and seemed delighted to accompany me back to assist the maiden who had fallen ill so early in her Spanish sojourn. When we arrived back in Aras de Alpuente, Chloe's condition was no better. I left the doctor alone with her and waited nervously in the next room. Ten minutes later, the doctor emerged.

'Ess nutting to worry about.'
'She'll be OK?'
'Yes, my friend, she'll be OK in the mornin'.'
'What was wrong with her?'
'Nutting much, a leetle stomach, a leetle head, ees very common among dee 'oliday makres. I give her peels. Really just a little anch-edonia in de head, wha you espect?'

6. Dr Saavedra had diagnosed a case of *anhedonia*, a disease defined by the British Medical Association as a reaction remarkably close to mountain sickness resulting from the sudden terror brought on by the threat of happiness. It was a common disease among tourists in this region of Spain, faced in these idyllic surroundings with the sudden realization that earthly happiness might be within their grasp, and

prey therefore to a violent physiological reaction designed to counteract such a daunting possibility.

7.   Because happiness is so terrifying and anxiety-inducing to accept, somewhat unconsciously, Chloe and I had always tended to locate *hedonia* either in memory or in anticipation. Though the pursuit of happiness was our avowed goal, it was accompanied by an implicit belief that it would be realized somewhere in the very distant future – a belief challenged by the felicity we had found in Aras de Alpuente and, to a lesser extent, in each other's arms.

8.   Why did we live this way? Perhaps because to enjoy ourselves in the present would have meant engaging ourselves in an imperfect or dangerously ephemeral reality, rather than hiding behind a comfortable belief in an afterlife. Living in the *future perfect tense* involved holding up an ideal life to contrast with the present, one that would save us from the need to commit ourselves to our situation. It was a pattern akin to that found in certain religions, in which life on earth is only a prelude to an ever-lasting and far more pleasant heavenly existence. Our attitude towards holidays, parties, work, and perhaps love had something immortal to it, as though we would be on the earth for long enough not to have to stoop so low as to think these occasions finite in number – and hence be forced to draw proper value from them.

9.   If Chloe had now fallen ill, was it not perhaps because the present was catching up with her dissatisfaction? The

present had, for a brief moment, ceased to lack anything the future might hold. But was I not just as guilty of the disease as Chloe? Had there not been many times when the pleasures of the present had been rudely passed over in the name of the future, love stories in which, almost imperceptibly, I had abstained from loving fully, comforting myself with the immortal thought that there would be other love affairs I would one day try to enjoy with the insouciance of men in magazines, future loves that would redeem my calamitous efforts to communicate with another whom history had set spinning on the earth at much the same time as me?

10. The future has some of the satisfactions and safety of the past. I recalled that as a child every holiday grew perfect only when I was home again, for then the anxiety of the present would make way for stable memories. I spent whole childhood years looking forward to the winter holidays, when the family took two weeks to go skiing in the Alps. But when I was finally on top of a slope, looking at pine-covered valleys below me and a fragile blue sky above, I felt a pervasive, existential anxiety that would then evaporate from the memory of the event, a memory that would be exclusively composed of the objective conditions (the top of a mountain, a fragile blue sky) and would hence be free of everything that had made the actual moment trying. The present was unpleasant not because I might have had a runny nose, or been thirsty, or forgotten a scarf, but because of my reluctance to accept that I was finally going to live out

a possibility that had all year resided in the comforting folds of the future. Yet as soon as I had reached the bottom of the slope, I would look back up the mountain and declare that it had been a perfect run. And so the skiing holiday (and much of my life generally) proceeded: anticipation in the morning, anxiety in the actuality, and pleasant memories in the evening.

11. There was for a long time something of this paradox in my relationship with Chloe: I would spend all day looking forward to a meal with her, would come away from it with the best impressions, but find myself faced with a present that had never equalled its anticipation or memory. It was one evening shortly before we'd left for Spain, on Will Knott's houseboat with Chloe and other friends, when, because everything was so perfect, I first grew unavoidably aware of my lingering suspicions towards the present moment. Most of the time, the present is too flawed to remind us that the disease of living in the *present imperfect tense* is within us, and nothing to do with the world outside. But that evening in Chelsea, there was simply nothing I could fault the moment on and hence had to realize that the problem lay within me: the food was delicious, friends were there, Chloe was looking beautiful, sitting next to me and holding my hand. And yet something was wrong all the same, the fact that I could not wait till the event had slipped into history.

12. The inability to live in the present lies in the fear of leaving the sheltered position of anticipation or memory, and

so of admitting that this is the only life that one is ever likely (heavenly intervention aside) to live. If commitment is seen as a group of eggs, then to commit oneself to the present is to risk putting all one's eggs in the present basket, rather than distributing them between the baskets of past and future. And to shift the analogy to love, to finally accept that I was happy with Chloe would have meant accepting that, despite the danger, all of my eggs were firmly in her basket.

13. Whatever pills the good doctor had given her, Chloe seemed completely cured the next morning. We prepared a picnic and went back to the lake, where we passed the day swimming and reading by the water. We spent ten days in Spain, and I believe (as much as one can trust memory) that for the first time, we both risked living those days in the present. Living in this tense did not always mean bliss. The anxieties created by love's unstable happiness routinely exploded into argument. I remember a furious row in the village of Fuentelespino de Moya, where we had stopped for lunch. It had started with a joke about an old girlfriend, and had grown into a suspicion in Chloe's mind that I was still in love with her. Nothing could have been further from the truth, yet I had taken such suspicion to be a projection of Chloe's own declining feelings for me and accused her of as much. By the time the arguing, sulking and reconciliations were over, it was mid-afternoon, and we were both left wondering what the tears and shouting had been about. There were other arguments. I remember one near the village of Losa del Obispo about whether or not we were bored with

one another, another near Sot de Chera that had started after I had accused Chloe of being an incompetent map reader and she had countered the charge by accusing me of 'road fascism'.

14. The reasons behind such arguments were never the surface ones: whatever Chloe's deficiencies with the *Guide Michelin*, or my intolerance to driving around in large circles through the Spanish countryside, what was at stake were far deeper anxieties. The strength of the accusations we made, their sheer implausibility, showed that we argued not because we hated one another, but because we loved one another too much – or, to risk confusing things, because we hated loving one another to the extent we did. Our accusations were loaded with a complicated subtext, *I hate you, because I love you*. It amounted to a fundamental protest, *I hate having no choice but to risk loving you like this*. The pleasures of depending on someone pale next to the paralysing fears that such dependence involves. Our occasionally fierce and somewhat inexplicable arguments during our trip through Valencia were nothing but a necessary release of tension that came from realizing that each one had placed all their eggs in the other's basket – and was helpless to aim for more sound household management. Our arguments sometimes had an almost theatrical quality to them, a joy and exuberance would manifest itself as we set about destroying the bookshelf, smashing the crockery, or slamming doors: 'It's nice being able to feel I can hate you like this,' Chloe once said to me. 'It reassures me that you can take it, that I can tell you to

fuck off and you'll throw something at me but stay put.' We needed to shout at one another partly to see whether or not we could tolerate each other's shouting. We wanted to test each other's capacity for survival: only if we had tried in vain to destroy one another would we know we were safe.

15. It is easiest to accept happiness when it is brought about through things that one can control, that one has achieved after much effort and reason. But the happiness I had reached with Chloe had not come as a result of any personal achievement or effort. It was simply the outcome of having, by a miracle of divine intervention, found a person whose company was more valuable to me than that of anyone else in the world. Such happiness was dangerous precisely because it was so lacking in self-sufficient permanence. Had I after months of steady labour produced a scientific formula that had rocked the world of molecular biology, I would have had no qualms about accepting the happiness that ensued from such a discovery. The difficulty of accepting the happiness Chloe represented came from my absence in the causal process leading to it, and hence my lack of control over the happiness-inducing element in my life. It seemed to have been arranged by the gods, and was consequently accompanied by all the primitive fear of divine retribution.

16. 'All of man's unhappiness comes from an inability to stay in his room alone,' said Pascal, advocating a need for man to build up his own resources over and against a debilitating dependence on the social sphere. But how could this

possibly be achieved in love? Proust tells the story of Mohammed II who, sensing that he was falling in love with one of the wives in his harem, at once had her killed because he did not wish to live in spiritual bondage to another. Short of this, I had long ago given up hopes of achieving self-sufficiency. I had gone out of my room, and begun to love another – thereby taking on the risk inseparable from basing one's life around another human being.

17. The anxiety of loving Chloe was in part the anxiety of being in a position where the cause of my happiness might so easily vanish, where she might suddenly lose interest, die, or marry another. At the height of love, there appeared a temptation to end the relationship prematurely, so that either Chloe or I could play at being the executioner, rather than see the other partner, or habit, or familiarity end things. We were sometimes seized by an urge (manifested in our arguments about nothing) to kill our love affair before it had reached its natural end, a murder committed not out of hatred, but out of an excess of love – or rather, out of the fear that an excess of love may bring. Lovers may kill their own love story only because they are unable to tolerate the uncertainty, the sheer risk, that their experiment in happiness has delivered.

18. Hanging over every love story is the thought, as horrible as it is unknowable, of how it will end. It is as when, in full health and vigour, we try to imagine our own death, the only difference between the end of love and the end of

life being that at least in the latter, we are granted the comforting thought that we will not feel anything *after* death. No such comfort for the lover, who knows that the end of the relationship will not necessarily be the end of love, and almost certainly not the end of life.

17

Contractions

1. Though questions of reality and falsehood in this area are notorious for resisting scrutiny and systematic analysis, after our return from Spain I began to suspect – without quite being able to look at the evidence in the face – that Chloe had started to simulate all or some of her orgasms.

2. Her customary behaviour was replaced by an exaggerated activity apparently designed to divert me from her lack of genuine involvement in the process. The change was not accompanied by any obvious sign of uninterest. Indeed, lovemaking as a whole became more passionate. Not only was it performed more often, it was also performed in different positions and at different hours of the day, it was more turbulent, there were screams, even crying, the gestures closer to anger than the gentleness normally associated with the act.

3. What should have been said to Chloe was eventually shared with a great male friend instead.
   'I don't know what's happening, Will, sex simply isn't what it used to be.'

'Don't worry, it goes in phases, you can't expect it to be high octane every time. Not even I expect that.'

'I just feel something else is wrong, I don't know what, but in the months since we came back from Spain, I've been noticing stuff. And I don't mean only in the bedroom, that's just a kind of symptom. I mean everywhere.'

'Like?'

'Well, nothing I could put a finger on directly. All right, here's one thing I remember. She likes a different cereal than me, but because I spend a lot of time at her place, she usually buys the kind of cereal I like so we can have breakfast together. Then all of a sudden last week, she stops buying it, and says it's too expensive. I don't want to come to any conclusions, I'm just noticing.'

4. Will and I were standing in the reception area of our office. A cocktail party was in progress to celebrate the firm's twentieth birthday. I had brought Chloe with me, for whom this was a first chance to see my work-space.

'Why does Will have so many more commissions than you?' Chloe asked Will and me after wandering around the exhibits.

'You answer that one, Will.'

'That's because real geniuses always have a hard time getting their work accepted,' answered Will, cancelling out what might have been a compliment through exaggeration.

'Your designs are brilliant,' Chloe told him, 'I've never seen anything so inventive, especially for office projects. The use of materials is just incredible, and the way you've managed to integrate the brick and metal so well. Couldn't you do things like that?' Chloe asked me.

'I'm working on a number of ideas, but my style is very different, I work with different materials.'

'Well, I think Will's work is great, incredible in fact. I'm so glad I came to see it.'

'Chloe, it's great to hear you say so,' answered Will.

'I'm so impressed, your work is exactly the kind of thing I'm interested in and I think it's such a pity that more architects don't do what you're trying to do. I imagine it can't be easy.'

'It's not that easy, but I've always been taught to go with the things I believe in. I build the houses that make me feel real, and then the people who live in them end up absorbing a kind of energy from them.'

'I think I see what you mean.'

'You'd see better if we were out in California. I was working on a project in Monterey, and I mean, there you'd really get a sense of what you can do by using different kinds of stone as well as some steel and aluminium, and working *with* the landscape instead of *against* it.'

5. It is part of good manners not to question the criteria responsible for eliciting another's love. The dream is that one has not been loved for criteria at all, but rather *for who one is*, an ontological status beyond properties or attributes. From within love, as within wealth, a taboo surrounds the means of acquiring and sustaining affection or property. Only poverty, either of love or money, leads one to question the

system – perhaps the reason why lovers do not make great revolutionaries.

6. Passing an unfortunate woman in the street one day, Chloe had asked me, 'Would you have loved me if I'd had an enormous birthmark on my face like she does?' The yearning is that the answer be 'yes' – an answer that would place love above the mundane surfaces of the body, or more particularly, its cruel unchangeable ones. *I will love you not just for your wit and talent and beauty, but simply because you are you, with no strings attached. I love you for who you are deep in your soul, not for the colour of your eyes or the length of your legs or size of your chequebook*. The longing is that the lover admire us stripped of our external assets, appreciating the essence of our being without accomplishments, ready to repeat the unconditional love said to exist in some parts between parent and child. The real self is what one can freely choose to be, and if a birthmark arises on our forehead or age withers us or recession bankrupts us, then we must be excused for accidents that have damaged what is only our surface. And even if we are beautiful and rich, then we do not wish to be loved on account of these things, for they may fail us, and with them, love. I would prefer you to compliment me on my brain than on my face, but if you must, then I would rather you comment on my smile (motor- and muscle-controlled) than on my nose (static and tissue-based). The desire is that I be loved even if I lose everything: leaving nothing but 'me', this mysterious 'me' taken to be the self at its weakest, most vulnerable point.

Do you love me enough that I may be weak with you? Everyone loves strength, but *Do you love me for my weakness?* That is the real test. *Do you love me stripped of everything that might be lost, for only the things I will have for ever?*

7. That evening at the architectural office, I first began to sense Chloe slipping away from me, losing admiration for my work and beginning to question my value in relation to other men. Because I was tired, and Chloe and Will were not, I went home and they chose to go on to the West End for a drink. Chloe told me she'd call as soon as she got home, but by eleven o'clock, I decided to call her. The answerphone replied, as it did when I called again at two thirty that morning. The urge was to confess my anxieties into the machine, but to formulate them seemed to bring them closer into existence, dragging a suspicion into the realm of accusation and counter-accusation. Perhaps it was nothing – or at least everything: I preferred to imagine her in an accident than playing truant with Will. I called the police at four in the morning, and asked them in the most responsible tone a man drunk on vodka may adopt, if they had not seen evidence, perhaps a mutilated body or wrecked Volkswagen, of my angel in a short green skirt and black jacket, last seen in an office near the Barbican. No, sir, no such sighting had been made, was she a relative or just a friend? Could I wait till morning, and contact the station again then?

8. '*One can think problems into existence,*' Chloe had told me. I dared not think, for fear of what I might find. The freedom

to think involves the courage to stumble upon our demons. But the frightened mind cannot wander, I stayed tethered to my paranoia, brittle as glass. Bishop Berkeley and later Chloe had said that if one shuts one's eyes, the outer world may be said to be no more real than a dream, and now more than ever the power of illusion came to seem comforting, the urge not to look truth in the face, the urge that if only one did not think, an unpleasant truth might not exist.

9. Feeling implicated in her absence, guilty for my suspicions, and angry at my own guilt, I pretended to have noticed nothing when Chloe and I met at ten o'clock the following day. Yet she must have been guilty – for why else would she have gone to her local supermarket to add to her kitchen the missing breakfast cereal to fill Weltschmertz's stomach? She accused herself not by her indifference, but by her sense of duty, a large packet of Three Cereal Golden Bran prominently placed on the window ledge.

'Is something wrong with it? Isn't that the one you like?' asked Chloe, watching me stumble over my mouthfuls.

10. She said she had stayed the night at her girlfriend Paula's house. Will and she had chatted till late in a bar in Soho, and as she'd had a bit to drink, it had seemed easier to stop off in Bloomsbury than make the journey back home to Islington. She had wanted to call me, but it would surely have woken me up. I had said I wanted to go to sleep early, so wasn't it the best thing? Why was I making that face? Did I want more milk to go with the three cereals?

11.   An urge accompanies epistemically stunted accounts of reality – the urge, if they are pleasant, to believe them. Like an optimistic simpleton's view of the world, Chloe's version of her evening was desirably believable, like a hot bath in which I wished to sit for ever. *If she believes in it, why shouldn't I? If it's this simple for her, why should it be so complicated for me?* I wished to be taken in by her story of a night spent on the floor of Paula's flat in Bloomsbury, able in that case to set aside my alternative evening (another bed, another man, unfaked pleasure). Like the voter from whom the politician's caramel promise draws a tear, I was lured by falsehood's ability to appeal to my deepest emotional yearning.

12.   Therefore, as she had spent the night with Paula, had bought cereal, and all was forgiven, I felt a burst of confidence and relief, like a man awaking from a nightmare. I got up from the table and put my arms around the beloved's thick white pullover, caressing her shoulders through the wool, then bending down to kiss her neck, nibbling at her ear, feeling the familiar perfume of her skin and the brush of her hair against my face. *'Don't, not now,'* said the angel. But, disbelieving, caught up in the familiar perfume of her skin and brush of hair against his face, Cupid continued to pucker his lips against her flesh. *'I said once already, not now!'* repeated the angel, so that even he might hear.

13.   The pattern of the kiss had been formed during their first night together. She had placed her head beside his and,

fascinated by this soft juncture between mind and body, he had begun running his lips along the curve of her neck. It had made her shudder and smile, she had played with his hand, and shut her eyes. It had become a routine between them, a signature of their intimate language. *Don't, not now.* Hate is the hidden script in the letter of love, its foundations are shared with its opposite. The woman seduced by her partner's way of kissing her neck, turning the pages of a book, or telling a joke watches irritation collect at precisely these points. It is as if the end of love was already contained in its beginning, the ingredients of love's collapse eerily foreshadowed by those of its creation.

14.   *I said once already, not now.* There are cases of skilled doctors, experts at detecting the first signs of cancer in their patients, who will somehow ignore the growth of football-sized tumours in their own body. There are examples of people who in most walks of life are clear and rational, but who are unable to accept that one of their children has died or that their wife or husband has left them – and will continue to believe the child has merely gone missing or the spouse will leave their new marriage for the old. The shipwrecked lover cannot accept the evidence of the wreckage, continuing to behave as though nothing had changed, in the vain hope that by ignoring the verdict of execution, death will somehow be stalled. The signs of death were everywhere waiting to be read – had I not been struck by the illiteracy pain had induced.

15. The victim of love's demise grows unable to locate original strategies to revive the corpse. At precisely the time when things might still have been rescued with ingenuity, fearful *and hence unoriginal*, I became nostalgic. Sensing Chloe drawing away, I attempted to pull her back through blind repetition of elements that had in the past cemented us. I continued with the kiss, and in the weeks thereafter, insisted that we return to cinemas and restaurants where we had spent pleasant evenings, I revisited jokes we had laughed at together, I readopted positions our bodies had once moulded.

16. I sought comfort in the familiarity of our in-house language, the language used to ease previous conflicts, a joke designed to acknowledge and hence render inoffensive the temporary fluctuations of love.

'Is something wrong today?' I asked one morning when Venus looked almost as pale and sad as I.

'Today?'

'Yes, today, is something wrong?'

'No, why? Is there any reason it should be?'

'I don't think so.'

'So why are you asking?'

'I don't know. Because you're looking a bit unhappy.'

'Sorry for being human.'

'I'm just trying to help. Out of ten today, what would you give me?'

'I really don't know.'

'Why not?'

'I'm tired.'

'Just tell me.'

'I can't.'

'Come on, out of ten. Six? Three? Minus twelve? Plus twenty?'

'I don't know.'

'Have a guess.'

'For Christ's sake, I don't know, leave me alone, damn it!'

17. The in-house language unravelled, it grew unfamiliar to Chloe, or rather, she feigned forgetting, so as not to admit denial. She refused complicity in the language, she played the foreigner, she began reading me against the grain, and found errors. I could not understand why things I was saying and that in the past had proved so attractive were now suddenly so irritating. I could not understand why, having not changed myself, I should now be accused of being offensive in a hundred different ways. Panicking, I embarked on an attempt to return to the golden age, asking myself, '*What had I been doing then that I perhaps am not doing now?*' I became a desperate conformist to a past self that had been the object of love. What I had failed to realize was that the past self was the one now proving so annoying, and that I was therefore doing nothing but accelerating the process towards dissolution.

18. I became an irritant, *one who has gone beyond caring for reciprocation*. I bought her books, I took her jackets to the dry cleaner's, I paid for dinner, I suggested we make a trip to Paris at Christmas time to celebrate our anniversary. But

humiliation could be the only result of loving against all evidence. She could sulk me, shout at me, ignore me, tease me, trick me, hit me, kick me, and still I would not react – and thereby grew abhorrent.

19.   At the end of a meal I had spent two hours preparing (largely taken up by an odd argument we fell into over Balkan history after Chloe began a peculiar defence of Serbian nationalism), I took Chloe's hand and told her, 'I just wanted to say, and I know it sounds sentimental, that however much we fight and everything, I still really care about you and want things to work out between us. You mean everything to me, you know that.'

Chloe (who had always read more psychoanalysis than fiction) looked at me suspiciously and replied, 'Listen, it's kind of you to say so, but it worries me; you've got to stop turning me into your ego ideal like this.'

20.   Things had reduced themselves to a tragicomic scenario: on the one hand, the man identifying the woman as an angel, on the other, the angel identifying love as something only a little short of a pathology.

18

Romantic Terrorism

1. *Why **don't** you love me?* is as impossible a question (though a far less pleasant one) to ask as *Why **do** you love me?* In both cases, we come up against our lack of conscious control in the amorous structure, the fact that love has been brought to us as a gift for reasons we never wholly determine or deserve. To ask such questions, we are forced to veer on one side towards complete arrogance, on the other to complete humility: *What have I done to deserve love?* asks the humble lover; I can have done nothing. *What have I done to be denied love?* protests the betrayed one, arrogantly claiming possession of a gift that is never one's due. To both questions, the one who hands out love can only reply: *Because you are you* – an answer that leaves the beloved dangerously and unpredictably strung between grandiosity and depression.

2. Love may be born at first sight, but it does not die with corresponding rapidity. Chloe must have feared that to talk or even leave would have been hasty, that she might have been opting for a life offering no more favourable alternative. It was hence a slow separation, the masonry of affect only

gradually prising itself loose from the loved one. There was guilt at the residual sense of responsibility towards a once-prized object, a form of treacly liquid left at the bottom of the glass that needed time to drain off.

3. When every decision is difficult, no decision is taken. Chloe prevaricated, I joined her (for how could any decision be pleasant for me?). We continued to see one another and sleep with one another. We even made plans to visit Paris at Christmas time, yet Chloe was curiously disengaged from the process, as though she were making arrangements for someone else – perhaps because it was easier to deal in air-line tickets than the issues that lay behind their purchase or non-purchase. Her apathy embodied the hope that by doing nothing, another might take the decision for her, that by displaying her indecision and frustration while not acting on it I would ultimately perform the move that she had needed (but been too scared) to make herself.

4. We entered the era of romantic terrorism.
    'Is there anything wrong?'
    'No, why, should there be?'
    'I just thought you might want to talk about things.'
    'What things?'
    'About us.'
    'You mean about you,' snapped Chloe.
    'No, I mean about us.'
    'Well, what about us?'
    'I don't know, really. It's just a sense I have that ever since

about the middle of September, we haven't really been communicating. It's like there's a wall between us and you're
refusing to acknowledge it's there.'

'I don't see a wall.'

'That's what I mean. You're even refusing to admit there
was ever anything other than this.'

'Than what?'

5. Once a partner has begun to lose interest, there is
apparently little the other can do to arrest the process. Like
seduction, withdrawal suffers under a blanket of reticence.
The very breakdown of communication is hard to discuss,
unless both parties have a desire to see it restored. This
leaves the lover in a desperate situation. Honest dialogue
seems to produce only irritation and smothers love in the
attempt to revive it. Desperate to woo the partner back
at any cost, the lover might at this point be tempted to
turn to romantic terrorism, the product of irredeemable
situations, a gamut of tricks (sulking, jealousy, guilt) that
attempt to force the partner to return love, by blowing up
(in fits of tears, rage or otherwise) in front of the loved one.
The terroristic partner knows he cannot realistically hope to
see his love reciprocated, but the futility of something is not
always (in love or in politics) a sufficient argument against
it. Certain things are said not because they will be heard,
but because it is important to speak.

6. When political dialogue has failed to resolve a grievance,
the injured party may also in desperation resort to terrorist

activity, extracting by force the concession it has been unable to seduce peacefully from its opposite number. Political terrorism is born out of deadlocked situations, behaviour that combines a party's need to act with an awareness (conscious or semi-conscious) that action will not go any way towards achieving the desired end – and will if anything only alienate the other party further. The negativity of terrorism betrays all the signs of childish rage, a rage at one's own impotence in the face of a more powerful adversary.

7. In May 1972, three members of the Japanese Red Army, who had been armed, briefed and financed by the Popular Front for the Liberation of Palestine (PFLP), landed on a scheduled flight at Lod Airport, near Tel Aviv. They disembarked, followed the other passengers into the terminal building, and once inside, pulled machine-guns and grenades out of their hand luggage. They began firing on the crowd indiscriminately, slaughtering twenty-four people and injuring a further seven before they were themselves killed by the security forces. What relation did such butchery have with the cause of Palestinian autonomy? The murders did not accelerate the peace process, they only hardened Israeli public opinion against the Palestinian cause, and in a final irony for the terrorists, it turned out the majority of their victims were not even Israelis, but belonged to a party of Puerto Rican Christians who had been on a religious pilgrimage to Jerusalem. Yet the action found its justification elsewhere, in the need to vent frustration in a cause where dialogue had ceased to produce results.

8.   Both of us could only spare a weekend in Paris, so we left on the last flight out of Heathrow on Friday, and planned to return late on the Sunday. Though we were going to France to celebrate our anniversary, it felt more like a funeral. When the plane landed in Paris, the airport terminal was sombre and empty. It had begun to snow and a fierce arctic wind was blowing. There were more passengers than taxis, so we ended up sharing a ride with a woman we had met at passport control, a lawyer travelling from London to Paris for a con-ference. Though the woman was attractive, I was in no mood to find her so, but nevertheless flirted with her as we made our way into the city. When Chloe attempted to join the conversation, I would interrupt her with a remark addressed exclusively (and seductively) to the woman. But success in inducing jealousy is dependent on a significant factor: the inclination of the targeted audience to give a damn. Hence terroristic jealousy is always a gamble: how far could I go in trying to make Chloe jealous? What if she were not to react? Whether she was merely hiding that jealousy so as to call my bluff (like politicians who appear on television and declare how unconcerned they are with the terrorist threat), or whether she genuinely did not care, I could not be sure. But one thing was certain, Chloe did not allow me the pleasure of a jealous reaction, and was more pleasant than she had been in a long time when we finally settled into our room in a small hotel on the Rue Jacob, perhaps cheered by the thought that I would, after all, get over her.

9.   Terrorists take a gamble in assuming that their actions

will prove terrifying enough to provide a form of bargaining power. There is the story of a wealthy Italian businessman who, late one afternoon, received a phone call in his office from a terrorist gang, telling him that they had kidnapped his youngest daughter. A huge sum was stipulated as ransom, and the threat levelled that if it wasn't paid, the daughter would never be seen alive again. But the businessman casually replied that, if they killed the girl, they would in fact be doing him a huge favour. He had ten children, he explained wearily, and they had all been a great disappointment and a trial to him, expensive to keep and the unfortunate result of only a few moments of exertion in the bedroom on his part. The ransom would not be paid, and if they wanted to kill her, that was their choice. And with that blunt message, the businessman put down the phone. Within hours, the girl was released.

10.   It was still snowing when we awoke the next morning, but it was too warm for it to settle, so the pavements turned to mud, brown beneath a low grey sky. We had decided to visit the Musée d'Orsay after breakfast, and planned to go on to a cinema in the afternoon. I had just shut the door to the hotel room, when Chloe asked me brusquely, 'Have you got the key?'

'No,' I answered, 'you told me a minute ago you had it.'

'Did I? No, I didn't,' said Chloe, 'I don't have the key. You've just locked us out.'

'I haven't locked us out. I shut the door thinking you had the key, because the key wasn't where I left it.'

'Well, that's really silly of you, because I don't have it either, so we're locked out – thanks to *you*.'

'Thanks to me! For Heaven's sake, stop blaming me for the fact that it was you who forgot the key.'

'I had nothing to do with the key.'

At that moment, Chloe turned towards the lifts, and (with novelistic timing) the room key fell out of her coat pocket onto the maroon carpet of the hotel.

'Oh, I'm sorry. I did have it all along, oh, well,' said Chloe.

But I decided I would not forgive her with ease, and snapped, 'That's it,' and headed for the stairs silently and melodramatically, Chloe calling after me, 'Wait, don't be silly, where are you going? I said I was sorry.'

11. A structurally successful terroristic sulk must be sparked by some wrong-doing, however small, on the part of the sulked, and yet is marked by a disproportion between insult inflicted and sulk elicited, drawing a punishment bearing little relation to the severity of the original offence – and one that cannot easily be resolved through normal channels. I had been waiting to sulk Chloe for a long time, but to begin sulking when one has not been wronged in any definite way is counter-productive, for there is a danger the partner will not notice and guilt not flourish.

12. I could briefly have shouted at Chloe, she back at me, and then our argument over the room key would have

unwound itself. At the basis of all sulks lies a wrong that might have been addressed and disappeared at once, but that instead is taken by the injured partner and stored for later and more painful detonation. Delays in explanations give grievances a weight that they would lack if the matter had been addressed as soon as it had arisen. To display anger shortly after an offence occurs is the most generous thing one may do, for it saves the sulked from the burgeoning of guilt and the need to talk the sulker down from his or her battlement. I did not wish to do Chloe such a favour, so I walked out of the hotel alone and headed towards Saint-Germain, where I spent two hours browsing in a series of bookshops. Then, instead of returning to the hotel to leave a message, I ate lunch alone in a restaurant, then went to see two films in a row, eventually returning to the hotel at seven o'clock in the evening.

13. The key point about terrorism is that it is primarily designed to attract attention, a form of psychological warfare with goals (for instance, the creation of a Palestinian state) unrelated to military techniques (opening fire in the arrival lounge of Lod Airport). There is a discrepancy between means and ends, a sulk being used to make a point relatively unconnected to the sulk itself – *I am angry at you for accusing me of losing the key* symbolizing the wider (but unspeakable) message *I am angry at you for no longer loving me.*

14. Chloe was no brute and, whatever I might claim, had

generous tendencies for self-blame. She had tried to follow me to Saint-Germain, but had lost me in the crowd. She had returned to the hotel, waited a while, and then gone to the Musée d'Orsay. When I finally came back to the room, I found her resting in bed, but without speaking to her, went into the bathroom and took a long shower.

15. The sulker is a complicated creature, giving off messages of deep ambivalence, crying out for help and attention, while at the same time rejecting it should it be offered, *wanting to be understood without needing to speak*. Chloe asked if she could be forgiven, saying she hated to leave arguments unresolved and wanted us to spend a pleasant anniversary evening that night. I said nothing. Unable to express the full extent of my anger with her (an anger that had nothing to do with a key), I had grown unreasonable. Why had it become so hard for me to say what I meant? Because of the danger of communicating my real grievance: that Chloe had ceased to love me. My hurt was so inexpressible, had so little to do with a forgotten key, that I would have looked like a fool to bring the matter up at this stage. My anger was hence forced underground. Unable to say directly what I meant, I resorted to symbolizing meaning, half hoping, half dreading that the symbol would be decoded.

16. After my shower, we finally made it up over the key incident, and went out for dinner to a restaurant on the Île de la Cité. We were both on best behaviour, keen to avoid tensions, chatting on neutral territory about books, films,

and capital cities. It might have seemed (from the waiter's point of view) that the couple was indeed a happy one – and that romantic terrorism had scored a significant victory.

17. Yet ordinary terrorists have a distinct advantage over romantic terrorists, the fact that their demands (however outrageous) do not include the most outrageous demand of all, the demand *to be loved*. I knew that the happiness we were enjoying that evening in Paris was illusory, because the love that Chloe was displaying had not been given spontaneously. It was the love of a woman who feels guilty for the fact she has ceased to feel affection, but who nevertheless attempts a display of loyalty (as much to convince herself as her partner). Hence my evening was not a happy one: my sulk had worked, but its success had been empty.

18. Though ordinary terrorists may occasionally force concessions from governments by blowing up buildings or school children, romantic terrorists are doomed to disappointment because of a fundamental inconsistency in their approach. *You must love me*, says the romantic terrorist, *I will force you to love me by sulking you or making you feel jealous*, but then comes the paradox, for if love is returned, it is at once considered tainted, and the romantic terrorist must complain, *If I have only forced you to love me, then I cannot accept this love, for it was not spontaneously given*. Romantic terrorism is a demand that negates itself in the process of its resolution, it brings the terrorist up against an uncomfortable reality – that love's death cannot be arrested.

19. As we walked back towards the hotel, Chloe slipped her hand in my coat pocket and kissed me on the cheek. I did not return her kiss, not because a kiss was not the most desired conclusion to a terrible day, simply because I could no longer feel Chloe's kiss to be genuine. I had lost the will to force love on its unwilling recipient.

19

Beyond Good and Evil

1. Early on Sunday evening, Chloe and I were sitting in the economy section of a British Airways jet, making our way back from Paris to London. We had recently crossed the Normandy coast, where a blanket of winter cloud had given way to an uninterrupted view of dark waters below. Tense and unable to concentrate, I shifted uncomfortably in my seat. There was something threatening about the flight, the dull background throb of the engines, the hushed grey interior, the candy smiles of the airline employees. A trolley carrying a selection of drinks and snacks was making its way down the aisle and, though I was both hungry and thirsty, it filled me with the vague nausea that meals may elicit in aircraft.

2. Chloe had been listening to her Walkman while dozing, but she now pulled out the plugs from her ears and stared with her large watery eyes at the seat in front of her.

    'Are you all right?' I asked.

    There was a silence, as though she had not heard. Then she spoke.

    'You're too good for me,' she said.

    'What?'

'I said, "You're too good for me." '

'What? Why?'

'Because you are.'

'What are you saying this for, Chloe?'

'I don't know.'

'If anything, I'd put it the other way round. You're always the one ready to make the effort when there's a problem, you're just more self-deprecating about your . . .'

'Shush, stop, don't,' said Chloe, turning her head away from me.

'Why?'

'Because I've been seeing Will.'

'*You've what?*'

'I've been seeing Will, OK.'

'What? What does *seeing* mean? *Seeing* Will?'

'For God's sake, I've been to bed with Will.'

'Would madam like a beverage or light snack?' enquired the stewardess, choosing this moment to introduce her wares.

'No, thank you.'

'Nothing at all, then?'

'No, I'm all right.'

'How about for sir?'

'No thanks, nothing.'

3. Chloe had started to cry.

'I can't believe this. I just cannot believe this. Tell me it's a joke, some terrible, horrible joke, you've been to bed with Will. When? How? How could you?'

'God, I'm so sorry, I really am. I'm sorry, but I . . . I . . . I'm sorry . . .'

Chloe was crying so hard, she was unable to speak. Tears were streaming down her face, her nose was running, her whole body shaken by spasms, her breathing halting, gasping. She looked in such pain, for a moment I forgot the import of her revelation, concerned only to stop the flow of her tears.

'Chloe, please don't cry, it's all right. We can talk about this. Tidge, please, take this handkerchief. It'll be OK, it will, I promise . . .'

'My God, I'm so sorry, God I'm sorry, you don't deserve this, you really don't.'

Chloe's devastation temporarily eased the burden of betrayal. Her tears represented a brief reprieve for my own. The irony of the situation was not lost on me – the lover comforting his beloved for the upset betraying him has caused her.

4. The tears might have drowned every last passenger and sunk the whole aeroplane had the captain not prepared to land soon after they had begun. It felt like the Flood, a deluge of sadness on both sides at the inevitability and cruelty of what was happening: it simply wasn't working, it was going to have to end. Things felt all the more lonely, all the more exposed in the technological environment of the cabin, with the clinical attentions of stewardesses, with fellow passengers staring with the smug relief others feel in the face of strangers' emotional crises.

5. As the plane pierced the clouds, I tried to imagine a
future: a period of life was coming brutally to an end, and
I had nothing to replace it with, only a terrifying absence.
We hope you enjoy your stay in London, and will choose to fly with
us again soon. To fly again soon, but would I live again soon?
I envied the assumptions of others, the security of fixed lives
and plans to take off again soon. What would life mean
from now on? Though we continued holding hands, I knew
how Chloe and I would watch our bodies grow foreign. Walls
would be built up, the separation would be institutional-
ized, I would meet her in a few months or years, we would be
light, jovial, masked, dressed for business, ordering a salad in
a restaurant – unable to touch what only now we could reveal,
the sheer human drama, the nakedness, the dependency, the
unalterable loss. We would be like an audience emerging
from a heart-wrenching play but unable to communicate
anything of the emotions they had felt inside, able only to
head for a drink at the bar, knowing there was more, but
unable to touch it. Though it was agony, I preferred this
moment to the ones that would come, the hours spent alone
replaying it, blaming myself and her, trying to construct a
future, an alternative story, like a confused playwright who
does not know what to do with his characters (save kill
them off for a neat ending . . .). All this till the wheels hit the
tarmac at Heathrow, the engines were thrown into reverse,
and the plane taxied towards the terminal, where it disgorged
its cargo into the immigration hall. By the time Chloe and
I had collected our luggage and passed through customs,
the relationship was formally over. We would try to be good

friends, we would try not to cry, we would try not to feel victims or executioners.

6. Two days passed, numb. To suffer a blow and feel nothing – in modern parlance, it means the blow must have been hard indeed. Then one morning, I received a hand-delivered letter from Chloe, her familiar black writing poured over two sheets of creamy-white paper:

> *I am sorry for offering you my confusion, I am sorry for ruining our trip to Paris, I am sorry for the unavoidable melodrama of it. I don't think I will ever cry again as much as I did aboard that miserable aeroplane, or be so torn by my emotions. You were so sweet to me, that's what made me cry all the more, other men would have told me to go to hell, but you didn't, and that's what made it so very difficult.*
>
> *You asked me in the terminal how I could cry and yet still be sure. You must understand, I cried because I knew it could not go on, and yet there was still so much holding me to you. I realize I cannot continue to deny you the love you deserve, but that I have grown unable to give you. It would be unfair, it would destroy us both.*
>
> *I shall never be able to write the letter which I would really want to write to you. This is not the letter I have been writing to you in my head for the last few days. I wish I could draw you a picture, I was never too good with a pen. I can't seem to say what I want, I only hope you'll fill in the blanks.*
>
> *I will miss you, nothing can take away what we have shared. I have loved the months we have spent together. It seems such a surreal combination of things, breakfasts, lunches, phone calls in mid-afternoon, late nights at the Electric, walks in*

Kensington Gardens. I don't want anything to spoil that. When you've been in love, it is not the length of time that matters, it's everything you've felt and done coming out intensified. To me, it's one of the few times when life isn't elsewhere. You'll always be beautiful to me, I'll never forget how much I adored waking up and finding you beside me. I simply don't wish to continue hurting you. I could not bear for it slowly all to go stale.

I don't know where I will go from here. I will perhaps spend time on my own over Christmas or spend it with my parents. Will is going to California soon, so we'll see. Don't be unfair, don't blame him. He likes you very much and respects you immensely. He was only a symptom, not the cause of what's happened. Excuse this messy letter, its confusion will probably be a reminder of the way I was with you. Forgive me, you were too good for me. I hope we can stay friends. All my love . . .

7.   The letter brought no relief, only reminders. I recognized the cadences and accent of her speech, carrying with it the image of her face, the smell of her skin – and the wound I had sustained. I wept at the finality of the letter, the situation confirmed, analysed, turned into the past tense. I could feel the doubts and ambivalence in her syntax, but the message was definitive. It was over, she was sorry it was over, but love had ebbed. At the end of a relationship, it is the one who is not in love who makes the tender speeches. I was overwhelmed by a sense of betrayal, betrayal because a union in which I had invested so much had been declared bankrupt without my feeling it to be so. Chloe had not given it a chance, I argued with myself, knowing the hopelessness of these inner courts announcing hollow verdicts at four

thirty in the morning. Though there had been no contract, only the contract of the heart, I felt stung by Chloe's disloyalty, by her heresy, by her night with another man. How was it morally possible this should have been allowed to happen?

8.   It is surprising how often rejection in love is framed in moral language, the language of right and wrong, good and evil, as though to reject or not reject, to love or not to love, was something that naturally belonged to a branch of ethics. It is surprising how often the one who rejects is labelled evil, and the one who is rejected comes to embody the good. There was something of this moral attitude in both Chloe's and my behaviour. Framing her rejection, she had equated her inability to love with evil, and my love for her as evidence of goodness – hence the conclusion, made on the basis of nothing more than that I still desired her, that I was 'too good' for her. Assuming that she largely meant what she said and was not simply being polite, she had made the ethical point that she was not good enough for me, by virtue of nothing more than having ceased to love me – something she had deemed made her a less worthy person than I, a man who, in all the goodness of his heart, still felt able to love her.

9.   But however unfortunate rejection may be, can we really equate loving with selflessness, and rejection with cruelty, can we really equate love with goodness and indifference with evil? Was my love for Chloe moral, and her rejection of me immoral? The guilt owed to Chloe for rejecting me depended primarily on the extent to which love could be

seen as something that I had given selflessly – for if selfish motives entered into my gift, then Chloe was surely justified in equally selfishly ending the relationship. Viewed from such a perspective, the end of love appeared to be a clash between two fundamentally selfish impulses, rather than between altruism and egoism, morality and immorality.

10. According to Immanuel Kant, a moral action is to be distinguished from an amoral one by the fact that it is performed out of duty and regardless of the pain or pleasure involved. I am behaving morally only when I do something without consideration of what I may get in return for it, when I am guided solely by duty: 'For any action to be morally good, it is not enough that it should conform to the moral law – it must also be done for the sake of the moral law.'* Actions performed as a result of disposition cannot count as moral, a direct rejection of the utilitarian view of morality based around inclination. The essence of Kant's theory is that morality is to be found exclusively in the *motive* from which an act is performed. To love someone is moral only when that love is given free of any expected return, if that love is given simply for the sake of giving love.

11. I called Chloe immoral because she had rejected the attentions of someone who had on a daily basis brought her comfort, encouragement, support, and affection. But was she

---

* *Groundwork of the Metaphysic of Morals*, Immanuel Kant (Harper Torchbooks, 1964).

to blame in a *moral* sense for spurning these? Blame is surely
due when we spurn a gift given at much cost and sacrifice,
but if the giver has derived as much pleasure from giving as
we derive from receiving, then is there really a case for using
moral language? If love is primarily given out of selfish
motivations (i.e. for one's own benefit even as it arises out of
the benefit of the other), then it is not, in Kantian eyes at
least, a moral gift. Was I better than Chloe simply because I
loved her? Of course not, for though my love for her included
sacrifices, I had made them because it made me happy to do
so, I had not martyred myself, I had acted only because it
accorded so perfectly with my inclinations, because it was
not a duty.

12.   We spend our time loving like utilitarians, in the bedroom we are followers of Hobbes and Bentham, not Plato and
Kant. We make moral judgements on the basis of preference,
not transcendental values. As Hobbes put it in his *Elements
of Law*:

> Every man calleth that which pleaseth and is delightful
> to him, good; and that evil which displeaseth him:
> insomuch that while every man differeth from other in
> constitution, they differ also one from another con-
> cerning the common distinction of good and evil. Nor
> is there such thing as *agathon haplos*, that is to say, simply
> good . . . *

---

* *Elements of Law*, Thomas Hobbes (ed. Molesworth, 1839–45).

13.   I had called Chloe evil because she 'displeaseth-ed' *me*, not because she was in herself inherently evil. My value system was a *justification* of a situation rather than an explanation of Chloe's offence according to an absolute standard. I had made the classic moralist's error, traced so succinctly by Nietzsche:

> First of all, one calls individual actions good or bad quite irrespective of their motives but solely on account of their useful or harmful consequences. Soon, however, one forgets the origin of these designations and believes that the quality good and evil is inherent in the actions themselves, irrespective of their consequences . . .*

What gave me pleasure and pain determined the moral labels I chose to affix to Chloe. I was an egocentric moralizer, judging the world and her duties within it according to my own interests. My moral code was a mere sublimation of my desires.

14.   At the summit of self-righteous despair, I asked, '*Is it not my right to be loved and her duty to love me?*' Chloe's love was indispensable, her presence in the bed beside me as important as freedom or the right to life. If the government assured me these two, why could it not assure me the right to love? Why did it place such an emphasis on the right to life and free speech when I didn't give a damn about either, without

---

*   *Human, all too Human*, Friedrich Nietzsche (University of Nebraska Press, 1986).

someone to lend that life meaning? What use was it to live if it was without love and without being heard? What was freedom if it meant the freedom to be abandoned?

15. But how could one possibly extend the language of rights to love, to force people to love out of duty? Was this not simply another manifestation of romantic terrorism, of romantic fascism? Morality must have its boundaries. It is the stuff of High Courts, not of salty midnight tears and the heart-wrenching separations of well-fed, well-housed, over-read sentimentalists. I had only ever loved selfishly, spontaneously, like a utilitarian. And if utilitarianism states an action is right only when it produces the greatest happiness for the greatest number, then the pain now involved both in loving Chloe and hers in being loved was the surest sign that our relationship had not simply grown amoral, but immoral.

16. It was unfortunate that anger could not be wedded to blame. Pain mobilized me to seek an offender, but responsibility could not be pinned on Chloe. I learnt that humans stood in a relation of negative liberty towards one another, duty-bound not to hurt others, but certainly not forced to love one another if they did not wish. A primitive belief made me feel that my anger entitled me to blame someone else, but I recognized that blame can only be linked to choice. One does not get angry with a donkey for not being able to sing, for the donkey's constitution never gave it a chance to do anything but snort. Similarly, one cannot blame

a lover for loving or not loving, for it is a matter beyond their choice and hence responsibility – though what makes rejection in love harder to bear than donkeys who can never sing is that one did once see the lover loving. One finds it easier not to blame the donkey for not singing because it never sang, but the lover loved, perhaps only a short while ago, which makes the reality of the claim *I cannot love you any more* all the harder to digest.

17. The arrogance of wanting to be loved had emerged only now it was unreciprocated – I was left alone with my desire, defenceless, beyond the law, shockingly crude in my demands: ***Love me!*** And for what reason? I had only the usual paltry, insufficient excuse: ***Because I love you . . .***

20

Psycho-Fatalism

1. Whenever something calamitous happens to us, we are led to look beyond everyday causal explanations in order to understand why we have been singled out to receive such terrible, intolerable punishment. And the more devastating the event, the more inclined we are to imbue it with a significance it does not objectively have, the more likely we are to slip into a brand of psychological fatalism. Bewildered and exhausted by grief, I suffocated on question marks: '*Why me? Why this? Why now?*' I scoured the past to look for origins, omens, offences, anything that might count as an explanation for the wound I had sustained.

2. I was forced to abandon the optimism of everyday life. I gave up television and the daily papers. I took time off work. I became obsessed by millennial disasters: the risks of earthquakes, floods, and avian flus. I felt the transience of everything, the illusions upon which civilizations are built. I saw in happiness a violent denial of reality. I looked commuters in the face and wondered why they were unbothered by their own meaninglessness. I understood the pain of history, a record of carnage enveloped in nauseous nostalgia.

I felt the arrogance of scientists and politicians, newscasters and petrol-station attendants, the smugness of accountants and gardeners. I linked myself to the great outcasts, I became a follower of Caliban and Dionysus, and all who had been reviled for looking pus-filled truth in the face. In short, I briefly lost my mind.

3. But did I have a choice? Chloe's departure had rocked my confidence in just about everything. I felt that I had lost the ability to control my own destiny and had witnessed a childish, petulant demon take charge of me, make me smile, encourage me to feel safe, and then smash me onto the rocks. I was a character in a narrative whose grander design I was helpless to alter. I repented for the arrogance of my previous faith in free will.

4. Once more I thought of destiny, once more I felt the almost divine nature of love. Both its arrival and departure, the first so beautiful, the second gruesome, reminded me that I was but a plaything for the games of Cupid and Aphrodite. Unbearably punished, I sought out my guilt. Unsure of quite what I had done, I confessed to everything. I tore myself apart looking for reasons: every insolence returned to haunt me, acts of ordinary cruelty and thoughtlessness – none of these had been missed by the gods, who had now chosen to wreak their terrible revenge on me.

5. The ancient myths were dead, of course. We don't tend to believe that gods direct our lives. Yet we have replaced

them with a strong belief that there are comparably mysterious inner forces which govern what happens to us: I had been psychologically cursed to be unhappy in love.

6. It was psychoanalysis that provided names for my demons. It explained that life often unfolds in ways that defy self-awareness. In the Freudian world, a man may consciously try to love a woman, but unconsciously he may be doing everything to drive her into another's arms. Now Chloe had left, a new interpretation of our love story came to mind. It was a story that had been doomed to fail, that had been chosen *because* it would fail, and because in its failure, it would repeat a classic and perversely satisfying pattern of family neurosis. When my own parents had divorced, I recalled my mother warning me that I should be careful not to fall into an unhappy relationship, because her mother had fallen into one, and her mother before that. Was this not a hereditary psychological curse? The curse of Freud was upon me.

7. The essence of a curse is that the person labouring under it cannot know of its existence. It is a secret code within the individual writing itself over a lifetime. Oedipus is warned by the Oracle that he will kill his father and marry his mother – but conscious warnings serve no purpose, they cannot defuse the ominous prognosis. Oedipus is cast out from home in order to avoid the Oracle's prediction, but nevertheless ends up marrying Jocasta. His story is told for him, not by him. The curse defies the will.

8. What curse did I labour under? Nothing other than an inability to enjoy happy relationships, possibly the greatest misfortune known to man in modern society. Exiled from the shaded grove of love, I would be compelled to wander the earth till the day of my death, unable to shake off my compulsion to make those I love flee from me. I sought a name for this evil, and one night, in tears, found it contained in a dictionary of psychoanalytic terms under the entry for *repetition compulsion*:

> . . . an ungovernable process originating in the uncon-
> scious. As a result of its actions, the subject deliberately
> places himself in distressing situations, thereby repeating
> an old experience, but he does not recall this prototype;
> on the contrary, he has the strong impression that the
> situation is fully determined by the circumstances of
> the moment.[*]

9. No philosophy is further from the thought that what happens to us is random than psychoanalysis (even to deny meaning is meaningful). I did not simply love Chloe *and then* she left me. I loved Chloe *in order that* she would leave me. Buried deep in my unconscious, a pattern had been forged, in the early months or years. The baby had driven away the mother, or the mother had left the baby, and now the man had recreated the same scenario, different actors but the same plot. It was not for the shape of her smile or the liveli-

---

[*] *The Language of Psychoanalysis*, J. Laplanche, J. B. Pontalis (Karnac Books, 1988).

ness of her mind that I had chosen Chloe. It was because the unconscious, the perverse casting director of my life, had recognized in her a suitable character to leave the stage after inflicting the requisite amount of suffering.

10. Unlike the curses of the Greek gods, psychological fatalism at least held out the promise that it could be escaped. Where id was, ego might be. Had I had the strength to rise from my bed, I might have made it to the couch, and there, like Oedipus at Colonnus, begun to build an end to my sufferings. But I was unable to summon the necessary sanity to make it out of the house and seek help. I was unable even to talk, I could not share my grief with others, hence it ravaged me. I lay curled on the bed, the blinds drawn, irritated by the slightest noise or light, unduly upset if the milk in the fridge was stale or a drawer failed to open first time. Watching everything slip out of my grasp, I concluded that the only way to regain at least a measure of control was to kill myself.

21

Suicide

1. The Christmas season arrived, bringing with it carol singers, cards of good will and the first snowfalls. Chloe and I had been due to spend the Christmas weekend at a small hotel in Yorkshire. The brochure sat on my desk: 'Abbey Cottage welcomes its guests to warm Yorkshire hospitality in exquisite surroundings. Sit by the open fire in the oak-beamed living room, take a walk along the moors, or simply relax and let us take care of you. A holiday at Abbey Cottage is everything you always wanted from a hotel – and more.'

2. Two days before Christmas and hours before my death, at five o'clock on a sombre Friday evening, I received a call from Will Knott:

'I thought I'd ring to say goodbye, I'm due to fly back to San Francisco on the weekend.'

'I see.'

'Tell me, how are things with you?'

'I'm sorry?'

'Is everything all right?'

'All right? Well, yes, you could put it that way.'

'I was sorry to hear about you and Chloe. It's really too bad.'

'I was happy to hear about you and Chloe.'

'You've heard. Yeah, it just worked out. You know how much I always liked her, and she gave me a call and told me you guys had split up, and things moved from there.'

'Well, it's fantastic, Will.'

'I'm glad to hear you say it. I don't want this to get between us or anything, because a great friendship is not something I like to throw away. I always hoped you two could patch things up, I think you would have been great together, it's a real pity, but anyway. What are you doing over Christmas?'

'Staying home, I think.'

'Looks like you're going to get a real snowfall here, time to bring out the skis, eh?'

'Is Chloe with you now?'

'Is she with me now? Yes, no, I mean, she isn't actually with me right now. She was here, but she's just gone off to the store actually, we were talking about Christmas crackers, and she said she loved them, so she's gone to buy some.'

'That's great, give her my regards.'

'I'm sure she'd be delighted to hear we spoke. You know she's coming with me to spend Christmas in California?'

'Is she?'

'Yeah, it'll be great for her to see it. We'll spend a couple of days with my parents in Santa Barbara, then maybe go for a few days to the desert or something.'

'She loves deserts.'

'That's right, that's what she told me. Well, listen, I'd better leave you to it, and wish you a happy holiday. I've got to start sorting my stuff out around here. I may be back in Europe next fall, but anyway, I'll give you a call, and see how you're doing . . .'

3. I went into the bathroom and took out every last tablet I had collected, and laid them out on the kitchen table. With a mixture of pills, several glasses of cough syrup, and whisky, I would have enough to end the whole charade. What more sensible reaction than this, to kill oneself after rejection in love? If Chloe really was my whole life, was it not normal that I should end that life to prove it was impossible without her? Was it not dishonest to be continuing to wake up every morning if the person I claimed was the meaning of existence was now buying Christmas crackers for a Californian architect with a house in the foothills of Santa Barbara?

4. My separation from Chloe had been accompanied by a thousand platitudinous sympathies from friends and acquaintances: it might have been nice, people drift apart, passion can't last for ever, better to have lived and loved, time will heal everything. Even Will managed to make it sound unexceptional, like an earthquake or a snowfall, something that nature sends to try us, and whose inevitability one should not think of challenging. My death would be a violent denial of normality – it would be a reminder that I would not forget as others had forgotten. I wished to escape the erosion and softening of time, I wished the pain to last

for ever only so as to be connected to Chloe via its burnt nerve endings. Only by my death could I assert the importance and immortality of my love, only through self-destruction could I remind a world grown weary of tragedy that love was a deadly serious matter.

5. It was seven o'clock, and the snow was still falling, starting to form a blanket over the city. It would be my shroud. The one reading this will be alive, but the author will be dead, I reflected as I penned my note. *It was the only way I could say I love you, I'm mature enough not to want you to blame yourself for this, you know how I feel about guilt. I hope you will enjoy California, I understand the mountains are very beautiful, I know you could not love me, please understand I could not live without your love . . .* The suicide text had gone through many drafts: a pile of scrapped notepaper lay beside me. I sat at the kitchen table, wrapped in a grey coat, with only the shivering of the fridge for company. Abruptly, I reached for a tub of pills and swallowed what I only later realized were twenty effervescent vitamin C tablets.

6. I imagined Chloe receiving a visit from a policeman shortly after my inert body had been found. I imagined the look of shock on her face, Will Knott emerging from the bedroom with a soiled sheet draped around him, asking, '*Is there anything wrong, darling?*' and she answering '*Yes, oh, God, yes!*' before collapsing into tears. The most terrible regret and remorse would follow. She would blame herself for not understanding me, for being so cruel, for being so

short-sighted. Had any other man been so devoted to her as to take his own life for her?

7.   A notorious inability to express emotions makes human beings the only animals capable of suicide. An angry dog does not commit suicide, it bites the person or thing that made it angry, but an angry human sulks in its room and later shoots itself leaving a silent note. Man is the symbolic, metaphorical creature: unable to communicate my anger, I would symbolize it in my own death. I would do injury to myself rather than injure Chloe, enacting by killing myself what I was suggesting she had done to me.

8.   My mouth was frothing now, orange bubbles breeding in its cavity and exploding as they came into contact with the air, spraying a light orange film over the table and the collar of my shirt. As I observed this acidic chemical spectacle silently, I was struck by the incoherence of suicide: I did not wish to *choose* between being alive or dead. I simply wished to show Chloe that I could not, metaphorically speaking, live without her. The irony was that death would be too literal an act to grant me the chance to see the metaphor read, I would be deprived by the inability of the dead (in a secular framework at least) to look at the living looking at the dead. What was the point of making such a scene if I could not be there to witness others witnessing it? In picturing my death, I imagined myself in the role of audience to my own extinction, something that could never really happen in reality, when I would simply be dead, and hence denied my ultimate

wish – namely, *to be both dead and alive*. Dead so as to be able to show the world in general, and Chloe in particular, how angry I was, and alive, so as to be able to see the effect that I had had on Chloe and hence be released from my anger. It was not a question of being or not being. My answer to Hamlet was to be *and* not to be.

9. Those who commit a certain kind of suicide perhaps forget the second part of the equation, they look at death as an extension of life (a kind of afterlife in which to watch the effect of their actions). I staggered to the sink and my stomach contracted out the effervescent poison. The pleasure of suicide was to be located not in the gruesome task of killing the organism, but in the reactions of others to my death (Chloe weeping at the grave, Will averting his eyes, both of them scattering earth on my walnut coffin). To have killed myself would have been to forget that I would be too dead to derive any pleasure from the melodrama of my own extinction.

22

The Jesus Complex

1.   If there is any benefit to be found in the midst of agony, it may perhaps lie in the ability of certain sufferers to take this misery as evidence (however perverse) that they are special. Why else would they have been chosen to undergo such titanic torment other than to serve as proof that they are different, *and hence presumably better*, than those who do not suffer?

2.   I could not stand to be alone in my flat over the Christmas period, so I checked into a room in a small hotel off the Bayswater Road. I took with me a small suitcase and a set of books and clothes, but I neither read nor dressed. I spent whole days in a white bathrobe, lying on top of the bed and flicking through the channels of the television, reading room-service menus and listening to stray sounds coming up from the street.

3.   There was at first very little to distinguish that noise from the general moan of the traffic below: car doors were screaming shut, lorries were grinding into first gear, a pneumatic drill was pounding the pavement. And yet above

all that, I began to identify a quite different sound, rippling through the thin hotel wall from somewhere near my head, at that time pressed against a copy of *Time* magazine crushed against a sebaceous headboard. It was becoming undeniable, however much one tried to deny it (and heaven knows one might), that the sound from the next door room was none other than that of the mating ritual of the human species. 'Fuck,' I thought, 'they're fucking!'

4. When a man hears others in the midst of such activity, there are certain attitudes one may reasonably expect him to adopt. If he is young and imaginative, he may willingly induce a process of identification with the male through the wall, constructing, with his poet's mind, an ideal of the fortunate woman – Beatrice, Juliet, Charlotte, Tess – whose screams he flatters himself to have induced. Or, if affronted by this objective recording of libido, he may turn away, think of England and raise the volume of the television.

5. But my reaction was remarkable only for its passivity – or, rather, I failed to push reaction any way beyond acknowledgement. Since Chloe had left, I had done little but acknowledge. I had become a man who, in every sense of the word, could not be surprised. Surprise is, we are told by psychologists, a reaction to the unexpected, but I had come to expect everything, and could hence be surprised by nothing.

6. What was passing through my mind? Nothing but a

certain song heard once on the radio in Chloe's car, with the
sun setting over the edge of the motorway:

> *I'm in love, sweet love,*
> *Hear me calling out your name, I feel no shame,*
> *I'm in love, sweet love,*
> *Don't you ever go away, it'll always be this way.*

I had grown intoxicated with my own sadness, I had reached
the stratosphere of suffering, the moment where pain gives
rise to the Jesus complex. The sound of the copulating couple
and the song from happier days coalesced in the giant tears
that had begun to flow at the thought of the misfortunes of
my existence. But for the first time, these were not angry,
scalding tears, rather the bitter-sweet taste of waters grown
tinged with the conviction that it was not I, but the people
who had made me suffer, who were so blind. I was elated, at
the pinnacle where suffering brings one over into the valley
of joy, the joy of the martyr, the joy of the Jesus complex. I
imagined Chloe and Will travelling through California,
I listened to requests of 'more' and 'harder' from next door
and grew drunk on the liquor of grief.

7. 'How great can one be if one is understood by everyone?' I asked myself, contemplating the fate of the Son of
God. Could I really continue to blame myself for Chloe's
inability to understand me? Her rejection was more a sign
of how myopic she was than of how deficient I might have
been. No longer was I necessarily the vermin and she the
angel. She had left me for a third-rate Californian Corbusian

because she was simply too shallow to understand. I began
to reinterpret her character, concentrating on sides I found
least pleasant. She was in the end very selfish, her charms
only a superficial veneer masking an unattractive nature. If
she seduced people into thinking she was adorable, it had
more to do with her amusing conversation and kind smile
than any genuine grounds for love. Others did not know
her the way I did and it was clear (though I had not realized
it originally) that she was inherently self-centred, rather
caustic, at times inconsiderate, often thoughtless, on occasion ungracious, when she was tired impatient, when she
wanted her own way dogmatic, and in her decision to reject
me both unreflective and tactless.

8.   Grown infinitely wise through suffering, I could forgive,
pity, and patronize her for her lack of judgement – and to
do so gave me infinite relief. I could lie in a lilac-and-green
hotel room and be filled with a sense of my own virtue and
greatness. I pitied Chloe for everything she could not understand, the infinitely wise seer who watches the ways of men
and women with a melancholic, knowing grin.

9.   Why was my complex, the perverse psychological trick
that turned every defeat and humiliation into its opposite, to
be named after Jesus? I might have identified my suffering
with that of Young Werther or Madame Bovary or Swann,
but none of these bruised lovers could compete with Jesus's
untainted virtue and his unquestionable goodness beside the
evil of those he tried to love. It was not just the weepy eyes

and sallow face attributed to him by Renaissance· artists that made him such an attractive figure, it was that Jesus was a man who was kind, completely just, *and* betrayed. The pathos of the New Testament, as much as of my own love story, arose out of the sad tale of a virtuous but misrepresented man, who preached the love of everyone for their neighbour, only to see the generosity of his message thrown back in his face.

10.   It is hard to imagine Christianity having achieved such success without a martyr at its head. If Jesus had simply led a quiet life in Galilee making commodes and dining tables and at the end of his life published a slim volume entitled *My Philosophy of Life* before dying of a heart attack, he would not have acquired the status he did. The agonizing death on the Cross, the corruption and cruelty of the Roman authorities, the betrayal by his friends, all these were indispensable ingredients for proof (more psychological than historical) that the man had God on his side.

11.   Feelings of virtue breed spontaneously in the fertile soil of suffering. The more one suffers, the more virtuous one must be. The Jesus complex was entangled in feelings of superiority, the superiority of the underdog who considers himself above his oppressors, with their tyranny and blindness. Ditched by the woman I loved, I exalted my suffering into a sign of greatness (lying collapsed on a bed at three in the afternoon), and hence protected myself from experiencing my grief as the outcome of what was at best a mundane

romantic break-up. Chloe's departure may have killed me, but it had at least left me in glorious possession of the moral high ground. I was a martyr.

12. The Jesus complex lay at opposite ends of the spectrum from Marxism. Born out of self-hatred, Marxism prevented me from becoming a member of any club that would have me. The Jesus complex still left me outside the club gates but, because it was the result of ample self-love, declared that I was not accepted into the club only because I was so special. Most clubs, being rather crude affairs, naturally could not appreciate the great, the wise, and the sensitive, who were to be left at the gates or dropped by their girl-friends. My superiority was revealed primarily on the basis of my isolation and suffering: *I suffer, therefore I am special. I am not understood, but for precisely that reason, I am worthy of greater understanding.*

13. In so far as it avoids self-hatred, one must have sympathy for the alchemy by which a weakness is turned into virtue – and the evolution of my pain towards a Jesus complex certainly implied a degree of mental good health. It showed that in the delicate internal balance between self-hatred and self-love, self-love was now winning. My initial response to Chloe's rejection had been a self-hating one, where I had continued to love Chloe while hating myself for failing to make the relationship work. But my Jesus complex had turned the equation on its head, now interpreting rejection as a sign that Chloe was worthy of contempt or at best pity

(that paragon of Christian virtues). The Jesus complex was nothing more than a self-defence mechanism, I had not wanted Chloe to leave me, I had loved her more than I had ever loved a woman, but now that she had flown to California, my way of accepting the unbearable loss was to reinvent how valuable she had been in the first place. It was clearly a lie, but honesty is sometimes more than we have strength for when, abandoned and desperate, we spend Christmas alone in a hotel room listening to the sound of orgasmic beatitude from next door.

23

Ellipsis

1. There is an Arabic saying that the soul travels at the pace of a camel. While most of us are led by the strict demands of timetables and diaries, our soul, the seat of the heart, trails nostalgically behind, burdened by the weight of memory. If every love affair adds a certain weight to the camel's load, then we can expect the soul to slow according to the significance of love's burden. By the time it was finally able to shrug off the crushing weight of her memory, Chloe had nearly killed my camel.

2. With her departure had gone all desire to keep up with the present. I lived nostalgically, that is, with constant reference to my life as it had been with her. My eyes were never really open, they looked backwards and inwards to memory. I would have wished to spend the rest of my days following the camel, meandering through the dunes of yesteryear, stopping at charming oases to leaf through images of happier days. The present held nothing for me, the past had become the only inhabitable tense. What could the present be next to it but a mocking reminder of the one

who was missing? What could the future hold beside yet more wretched absence?

3.   When I was able to drown myself in memory, I would sometimes lose sight of the present without Chloe, hallucinating that the break-up had never occurred and that we were still together, as though I could have called her up at any time and suggested a film at the Odeon or a walk through the park. I would choose to ignore that she had decided to settle with Will in a small town in southern California, the mind would slip from factual reporting into a fantasy of the idyllic days of elation and laughter. Then, all of a sudden, something would throw me violently back into the Chloe-less present. The phone would ring and on my way to pick it up I would notice (as if for the first time, and with all the pain of that initial realization) that the place in the bathroom where Chloe used to leave her hairbrush was now empty. And the absence of that hairbrush would be like a stab in the heart, an unbearable reminder that she had left.

4.   The difficulty of forgetting her was compounded by the survival of so much of the external world that we had shared together, and in which she was still entwined. Standing in my kitchen, the kettle might suddenly release the memory of Chloe filling it up, a tube of tomato paste on a supermarket shelf might by a form of bizarre association remind me of a similar shopping trip months before. Driving across the Hammersmith flyover late one evening, I recalled driving down the same road on an equally rainy night but with Chloe

next to me in the car. The arrangement of pillows on my sofa evoked the way she placed her head down on them when she was tired, the dictionary on my bookshelf was a reminder of her passion for looking up words she did not know. At certain times of the week when we had tradition-ally done things together, there was an agonizing parallel between the past and present: Saturday mornings would bring back our gallery expeditions, Friday nights certain clubs, Monday evenings certain television programmes . . .

5. The physical world refused to let me forget. Life is crueller than art, for the latter usually assures that physical surroundings reflect characters' mental states. If someone in a García Lorca play remarks on how the sky has turned low, dark, and grey, this is no longer an innocent meteorologi-cal observation, but a symbol of a psychological state. Life gives us no such handy markers – a storm comes, and far from this being a harbinger of death and collapse, during its course, a person discovers love and truth, beauty and happiness, the rain lashing at the windows all the while. Similarly, in the course of a beautiful warm summer day, a car momentarily loses control on a winding road and crashes into a tree fatally injuring its passengers.

6. The external world did not follow my inner moods, the buildings that had provided the backdrop to my love story and that I had animated with feelings derived from it now stubbornly refused to change their appearance so as to reflect my inner state. The same trees lined the approach

to Buckingham Palace, the same stuccoed houses fronted the residential streets, the same Serpentine flowed through Hyde Park, the same sky was lined with the same porcelain blue, the same cars drove through the same streets, the same shops sold much the same goods to much the same people.

7. This refusal of change was a reminder that the world was an entity that would spin on regardless of whether I was in love or out of it, happy or unhappy, alive or dead. It could not be expected to change its expressions according to my moods, nor would the great blocks of stones that formed the streets of the city take time to consider my love story. Though they had been happy to accommodate my happiness, they had better things to do than to come crashing down now that Chloe was gone.

8. Then, inevitably, I began to forget. A few months after breaking up with her, I found myself in the area of London in which she had lived and noticed that the thought of her had lost much of the agony it had once held, I even noticed that I was not primarily thinking of her (though this was exactly her neighbourhood), but of the appointment that I had made with someone in a restaurant nearby. I realized that Chloe's memory had neutralized itself and become a part of history. Yet guilt accompanied this forgetting. It was no longer her absence that wounded me, but my growing indifference to it. Forgetting, however calming, was also a reminder of infidelity to what I had at one time held so dear.

9. There was a gradual reconquering of the self, new habits were created and a Chloe-less identity built up. My identity had for so long been forged around 'us' that to return to the 'I' involved an almost complete reinvention of myself. It took a long time for the hundreds of associations that Chloe and I had accumulated together to fade. I had to live with my sofa for months before the image of her lying on it in her dressing-gown was replaced by another image, the image of a friend reading a book on it, or of my coat lying across it. I had to walk through Islington on numberless occasions before I could forget that Islington was not simply Chloe's district, but a useful place to shop or have dinner. I had to revisit almost every physical location, rewrite over every topic of conversation, replay every song and every activity that she and I had shared in order to reconquer them for the present, in order to defuse their associations. But gradually I forgot.

10. My time with Chloe folded in on itself, like an accordion that contracts. My love story was like a block of ice gradually melting as I carried it through the present. The process was like a film camera which had taken a thousand frames a minute, but was now discarding most of them, selecting according to mysterious whims, landing on a certain frame because an emotional state had coalesced around it. Like a century that is reduced and symbolized by a certain pope or monarch or battle, my love affair refined itself to a few iconic elements (more random than those of historians but equally selective): the look on Chloe's face as we kissed

for the first time, the light hairs on her arm, an image of her standing waiting for me in the entrance to Liverpool Street Station, her white pullover, her laugh when I told her my joke about the Russian in a train through France, her way of running her hand through her hair . . .

11. The camel became lighter and lighter as it walked through time, it kept shaking memories and photos off its back, scattering them over the desert floor and letting the wind bury them in the sand, and gradually the camel became so light that it could trot and even gallop in its own curious way – until one day, in a small oasis that called itself the present, the exhausted creature finally caught up with the rest of me.

24

Love Lessons

1. We must assume that there are certain lessons to be drawn from love, or else we remain happy to repeat our errors indefinitely, like flies that drive themselves insane butting their heads against windowpanes, unable to understand that though the glass may look clear it cannot be flown through. Are there not certain basic truths to be learnt, shreds of wisdom that could prevent some of the excessive enthusiasms, the pain and the bitter disappointments? Is it not a legitimate ambition to become wise about love, in the way that one may become wise about diet, death, or money?

2. We start trying to be wise when we realize that we are not born knowing how to live, but that life is a skill that has to be acquired, like riding a bicycle or playing the piano. But what does wisdom counsel us to do? It tells us to aim for tranquillity and inner peace, a life free from anxiety, fear, idolatry, and harmful passions. Wisdom teaches us that our first impulses may not always be true, and that our appetites will lead us astray if we do not train reason to separate vain from genuine needs. It tells us to control our imagination or it will distort reality and turn mountains into molehills and

frogs into princesses. It tells us to hold our fears in check, so that we can be afraid of what will harm us, but not waste our energies fleeing shadows on the wall. It tells us we should not fear death, and that all we have to fear is fear itself.

3. But what does wisdom say about love? Is it something that should be given up completely, like coffee or cigarettes, or is it allowed on occasions, like a glass of wine or a bar of chocolate? Is love directly opposed to everything that wisdom stands for? Do sages lose their heads or only overgrown children?

4. If certain wise thinkers have given a nod of approval to love, they have been careful to draw distinctions between its varieties, in much the way that doctors counsel against mayonnaise, but allow it when it is made with low-fat ingredients. They distinguish the rash love of a Romeo and Juliet from Socrates' contemplative worship of the Good, they contrast the excesses of a Werther with the brotherly love suggested by Jesus.

5. The difference could be grouped into categories of mature and immature love. Preferable in almost every way, the philosophy of mature love is marked by an active awareness of the good and bad within each person, it is full of temperance, it resists idealization, it is free of jealousy, masochism, or obsession, it is a form of friendship with a sexual dimension, it is pleasant, peaceful, and reciprocated (and perhaps explains why most people who have known the

wilder shores of desire would refuse its painlessness the title of *love*). Immature love on the other hand (though it has little to do with age) is a story of chaotic lurching between idealization and disappointment, an unstable state where feelings of ecstasy and beatitude combine with impressions of drowning and fatal nausea, where the sense that one has finally found *the answer* comes together with the feeling that one has never been so lost. The logical climax of immature (because absolute) love comes in death, symbolic or real. The climax of mature love comes in marriage, and the attempt to avoid death via routine (the Sunday papers, trouser presses, remote-controlled appliances). For immature love accepts no compromise, and once we refuse compromise, we are on the road to some kind of cataclysm.

6. With the naive common sense that complex problems may elicit, I would sometimes ask (as though the answer could fit on the back of an envelope), 'Why can't we just all love one another?' Surrounded on every side by the agonies of love, by the complaints of mothers, fathers, brothers, sisters, friends, and soap-opera stars, I would hold out the hope that simply because everyone was inflicting and suffering from much the same pain, a common answer could be found – a metaphysical solution to the world's romantic problems on the grandiose scale of the Communists' answer to the inequities of international capital.

7. I was not alone in my utopian daydream, joined there by a group of people, let me call them *romantic positivists*,

who believed that with enough thought and therapy, love could be made into a less painful, indeed almost healthy, experience. This assortment of analysts, preachers, gurus, therapists, and writers, while acknowledging that love was full of problems, supposed that genuine problems must have equally genuine solutions. Faced with the misery of most emotional lives, romantic positivists would try to identify causes – a self-esteem complex, a father complex, a mother complex, a complex complex – and suggest remedies (regression therapy, a reading of the *City of God*, gardening, meditation). Hamlet's fate could have been avoided with the help of a good Jungian analyst, Othello could have got his aggression out on a therapeutic cushion, Romeo might have met someone more suitable through a dating agency, Oedipus could have shared his problems in family therapy.

8.   Whereas art has a morbid obsession with the problems that attend love, romantic positivists throw the focus on the very practical steps that can be taken to prevent the most common causes of anguish and heartache. Next to the pessimistic views of much of Western romantic literature, romantic positivists appear as brave champions of a more enlightened and confident approach in an area of human experience traditionally left to the melancholy imagination of degenerate artists and psychotic poets.

9.   Shortly after Chloe left, I came across a classic of romantic positivist literature on a stand in a station bookshop, a

work by a certain Dr Peggy Nearly that went by the title of
The Bleeding Heart.* Though in a hurry to get back to my
office, I bought the book nevertheless, attracted by a notice
on its pink back cover that asked, 'Must being in love always
mean being in pain?' Who was this Dr Peggy Nearly, a
woman who could boldly claim to answer such a riddle?
From the first page of the book, I learnt that she was

> . . . a graduate of the Oregon Institute of Love and
> Human Relations, currently living in the San Francisco
> area, where she practises psychoanalysis, child therapy,
> and marriage counselling. She is the author of numer-
> ous works on emotional addiction, as well as penis envy,
> group dynamics, and agoraphobia.

10.   And what was *The Bleeding Heart* about? It told the
unfortunate yet optimistic story of men and women who fell
in love with unsuitable partners, those who would treat them
cruelly or leave them emotionally unfulfilled, take to drink
or become violent. These people had made an unconscious
connection between love and suffering, and could not stop
hoping that the unsuitable types they had chosen to adore
would change and love them properly. Their lives would be
ruined by the delusion that they could reform people who
were by nature incapable of answering their emotional needs.
By the third chapter, Dr Nearly had identified the roots of
the problem as lying in deficient parents, who had given
these unfortunate romantics a warped understanding of the

---

* *The Bleeding Heart*, Peggy Nearly (Capulet Books, 1987).

affective process. If they had never loved people who were nice to them, it was because their earliest emotional attachments had taught them that love should be unreciprocated and cruel. But by entering therapy and being able to work through their childhood, they might understand the roots of their masochism, and learn that their desire to change unsuitable partners was only the relic of a more infantile fantasy to convert their parents into proper care-givers.

11.   Perhaps because I had finished reading it only a few days before, I found myself drawing an unlikely parallel between the plight of those described by Dr Nearly and the heroine of Flaubert's great novel, the tragic Emma Bovary. Who was Emma Bovary? She was a young woman living in the French provinces, married to an adoring husband whom she loathed because she had come to associate love with suffering. Consequently, she began to have adulterous affairs with unsuitable men, cowards who treated her cruelly and could not be depended upon to fulfil her romantic longings. Emma Bovary was ill because she could not stop hoping that these men would change and love her properly – when it was obvious that Rodolphe and Léon considered her as nothing more than an amusing distraction. Unfortunately, Emma lacked the opportunity to enter therapy and become self-conscious enough to realize the origins of her masochistic behaviour. She neglected her husband and child, squandered the family money, and in the end killed herself with arsenic, leaving behind a young child and a distraught husband.

12. It is sometimes interesting to think how differently events in the past might have unfolded had certain contemporary solutions been available. What if Madame Bovary had been able to discuss her problem with Dr Nearly? What if romantic positivism had had a chance to intervene in one of literature's most tragic love stories? One wonders at how the conversation would have flowed had Emma walked into Dr Nearly's San Francisco clinic.

(Bovary on the couch, sobbing.)
NEARLY: Emma, if you want me to help you, you'll have to explain what's wrong.
(Without looking up, Madame Bovary blows her nose into an embroidered handkerchief.)
NEARLY: Crying is a positive experience, but I don't think we should be spending the entire fifty minutes on it.
BOVARY: *(speaking through her tears)* He didn't write, he didn't . . . write.
NEARLY: Who didn't write, Emma?
BOVARY: Rodolphe. He didn't write, he didn't write. He doesn't love me. I am a ruined woman. I am a ruined pathetic, miserable, childish woman.
NEARLY: Emma, don't speak this way. I've told you already, you must learn to love yourself.
BOVARY: Why compromise by loving someone that stupid?
NEARLY: Because you are a beautiful person. And it's because you don't see it that you are addicted to men who inflict emotional pain.
BOVARY: But it was so good at the time.
NEARLY: What was?
BOVARY: Being there, with him beside me, making love to

him, feeling his skin next to mine, riding through the
woods. I felt so real, so alive, and now my life is in
ruins.

NEARLY: Maybe you felt alive, but only because you knew it
couldn't last, that this man didn't really love you. You hate
your husband because he listens to everything you say, but
you can't stop falling in love with the sort of man who will
take two weeks to answer a letter. Quite frankly, Emma,
your view of love betrays evidence of compulsion and
masochism.

BOVARY: Does it? What do I know? I don't care if it's all a
sickness, all I want is to kiss him again, to feel him holding
me in his arms, to smell the perfume of his skin.

NEARLY: You have to start to make an effort to look inside
yourself, to go over your childhood, then perhaps you will
learn that you don't deserve all this pain. It's only because
you grew up in a dysfunctional family in which your
emotional needs were not met that you are stuck in this
pattern.

BOVARY: My father was a simple farmer.

NEARLY: Perhaps, but he was also emotionally unreliable,
so that you now respond to an unmet need by falling
in love with a man who can't give you what you really
want.

BOVARY: It's Charles that's the problem, not Rodolphe.

NEARLY: Well, my dear, we'll have to go on with this next
week. It's coming to the end of your session.

BOVARY: Oh, Dr Nearly, I meant to explain earlier, but I won't
be able to pay you this week.

NEARLY: This is the third time you tell me this sort of thing.

BOVARY: I apologize, but money is such a problem at the

moment, I am so unhappy, I find myself spending it all on shopping. Just today, I went and bought three new dresses, a painted thimble, and a china tea set.

13.   It is hard to imagine a happy end to Madame Bovary's therapy, or indeed a much happier end to her life. It takes a fervent romantic positivist to believe that Dr Nearly (if she was ever paid) could have converted Emma into the well-adjusted, uncompulsive, and caring wife that would have turned Flaubert's book into an optimistic tale of redemption through self-knowledge. Certainly Dr Nearly had an *interpretation* of Madame Bovary's problem, but there is a great difference between identifying a problem and solving it, between wisdom and the wise life. We are all more intelligent than we are capable, and awareness of the insanity of love has never saved anyone from the disease. Perhaps the concept of wise or wholly painless love is as much of a contradiction as that of a bloodless battle – Geneva Conventions aside, it simply cannot exist. The confrontation between Madame Bovary and Peggy Nearly is the confrontation between romantic tragedy and romantic positivism. It is the confrontation between wisdom and wisdom's opposite, which is not the ignorance of wisdom (that is easy to put right), but the inability to act on the knowledge of what one knows is right. Knowing the unreality of our affair had proved to be of no help to Chloe and me, knowing we might be fools had not turned us into sages.

14.   Rendered pessimistic by the intractable pains of love,

I decided to turn away from it altogether. If romantic positivism could be of no help, then the only valid wisdom was the stoic advice never to fall in love again. I would henceforth retreat from the world, see no one, live frugally, and throw myself into austere study. I read with admiration stories of men and women who had escaped earthly distractions, made vows of chastity, and spent their lives in monasteries and nunneries. There were stories of hermits who had endured life in caves in the desert for forty or fifty years, living only off roots and berries, never talking or seeing other human beings.

15. But sitting at a dinner party one evening, lost in Rachel's eyes while she outlined the course of her office life for me, I was shocked to realize how easily I might abandon a stoic philosophy in order to repeat all the mistakes I had lived through with Chloe. If I continued to look at Rachel's hair tied elegantly in a bun, or at the grace with which she used her knife and fork or the richness of her blue eyes, I knew I would not survive the evening intact.

16. The sight of Rachel alerted me to the limits of the stoic approach. Though love might never be painless and was certainly not wise, neither could it be forgotten. It was as inevitable as it was unreasonable – and its unreason was unfortunately no argument against it. Was it not absurd to retreat into the Judaean hills in order to eat roots and shoots? If I wanted to be courageous, were there not greater opportunities for heroism in love? Moreover, for all the

sacrifices demanded by the stoic life, was there not something cowardly within it? At the heart of stoicism lay the desire *to disappoint oneself before someone else had the chance to do so*. Stoicism was a crude defence against the dangers of the affections of others, a danger that it would take more endurance than a life in the desert to be able to face. In calling for a monastic existence free of emotional turmoil, stoicism was simply trying to deny the legitimacy of certain potentially painful yet fundamental human needs. However brave, the stoic was in the end a coward at the point of perhaps the highest reality, at the moment of love.

17.   We can always blind ourselves to the complexities of a problem by suggesting solutions that reduce the issue to a lowest common denominator. Both romantic positivism and stoicism were inadequate answers to the problems raised by the agonies of love, because both of them collapsed the question rather than juggling with its contradictions. The stoics had collapsed the pain and irrationality of love into a conclusive argument against it – thereby failing to balance the undoubted trauma of our desires with the intractability of our emotional needs. On the other hand, the romantic positivists were guilty of collapsing a certain easy grasp of psychological wisdom into a belief that love could be rendered painless for all, if only we learnt to love ourselves a little more – thereby failing to juggle a need for wisdom with the inherent difficulties of acting on its precepts, reducing the tragedy of Madame Bovary to an illustration of Dr Nearly's truistic theories.

18. I realized that a more complex lesson needed to be drawn, one that could play with the incompatibilities of love, juggling the need for wisdom with its likely impotence, juggling the idiocy of infatuation with its inevitability. Love had to be appreciated without flight into dogmatic optimism or pessimism, without constructing a philosophy of one's fears, or a morality of one's disappointments. Love taught the analytic mind a certain humility, the lesson that however hard it struggled to reach immobile certainties (numbering its conclusions and embedding them in neat series), analysis could never be anything but flawed – and therefore never stray far from the ironic.

19. Such lessons appeared all the more relevant when Rachel accepted my invitation for dinner the following week, and the very thought of her began sending tremors through the region the poets have called the heart, tremors that I knew could have meant one thing only – that I had once more begun to fall.

ALAIN DE BOTTON is the author of seven bestselling books, including *The Architecture of Happiness*, *How Proust Can Change Your Life*, *The Consolations of Philosophy*, and *The Art of Travel*. *Essays in Love* is his first book. He was born in 1969 and lives in London.

For more information, visit:
www.alaindebotton.com